BRITISH MEDICAL BULLETIN

VOLUME 52   NUMBER 2   APRIL 1996

Euthanasia: death, dying and the medical duty

Scientific Editors

G R Dunstan and P J Lachmann

PUBLISHED FOR THE BRITISH COUNCIL BY
THE ROYAL SOCIETY OF MEDICINE PRESS LIMITED

ROYAL SOCIETY OF MEDICINE PRESS LIMITED
1 Wimpole Street, London W1M 8AE, UK
150 East 58th Street, New York, NY 10155, USA

British Library Cataloguing in Publication Data
A catalogue record for this book is available from the British Library
ISBN 1-85315-278-1
ISSN 0007-1420

Subscription information: *British Medical Bulletin* is published quarterly in January,
April, July and October on behalf of the British Council by Royal Society of Medicine
Press Limited. Subscription rates for Volume 52 (1996) are £134 Europe (including UK),
US$222 USA, £137 elsewhere, £70 developing countries. Prices include postage by
surface mail within Europe, by air freight and second class post within the USA*, and by
various methods of air-speeded delivery to all other countries. Subscription orders and
enquiries should be sent to: Publications Subscription Department, Royal Society of
Medicine Press Limited, 1 Wimpole Street, London W1M 8AE, UK (Tel +44 (0)171 290
2928; Fax +44 (0)171 290 2929).
*Second class postage paid at Rahway, NJ. US Postmaster: Send address changes to *British Medical
Bulletin*, c/o Mercury Airfreight International Ltd Inc, 2323 Randolph Avenue, Avenel, NJ 07001,
USA.

Single copies (cased) of issues published from 1996 are available at £45/US$73 and may
be ordered from the Domus Medica, Royal Society of Medicine, 1 Wimpole Street,
London W1M 8AE, UK (Tel +44 (0)171 290 2960; Fax +44 (0)171 290 2969), from
booksellers, or directly from the distributors: Hoddle Doyle Meadows Limited, Station
Road, Linton, Cambs CB1 6UX, UK (Tel +44 (0)1223 893855; Fax +44 (0)1223
893852).

Back numbers (pre-1996): Orders for any title published prior to 1996 should be sent to
Pearson Professional Ltd, PO Box 77, Harlow, Essex CM19 5BQ, UK

This journal is indexed, abstracted and/or published online in the following media:
Adonis, Biosis, BRS Colleague (full text), Chemical Abstracts, Colleague (Online),
Current Awareness in Biological Science, Current Contents/Clinical Medicine, Current
Contents/Life Sciences, Excerpta Medica/Embase, Index Medicus/Medline, Medical
Documentation Service, Reference Update, Research Alert, Science Citation Index,
Scisearch, SIIC-Database Argentina, UMI (Microfilms)

Phototypeset by Dobbie Typesetting Limited, Tavistock, Devon
Printed in Great Britain by Henry Ling Limited, The Dorset Press, Dorchester

BRITISH MEDICAL BULLETIN   Volume 52   Number 2   April 1996

Euthanasia: death, dying and the medical duty

Scientific Editors

G R Dunstan and P J Lachmann

Acknowledgements

The committee that planned this number of the *British Medical Bulletin* was chaired by Professor Andrew Grubb and included Professor Gordon Dunstan, Professor Sjef Gevers, Dr Raanan Gillon and Professor Margot Jefferys.

The British Council and Royal Society of Medicine Press are most grateful to them for their help and advice, and particularly to Professors Gordon Dunstan and Peter Lachmann for their work as Scientific Editors.

Preface

The general plan of this book, as of other issues of the *British Medical Bulletin*, was the product of a few minds brought together by an officer of The British Council. The book was designed to take its place in a respected series of medical volumes.

Voluntary euthanasia is understood to mean the deliberate and intentional hastening of death at the request of the patient. It is now widely debated in society, and practised in some countries. But it is not a social question only. It is a question for the medical profession also because doctors are normally assumed to be the obvious people to give the lethal treatment. Indeed, it is difficult to imagine otherwise, unless society were to employ a panel of non-medical executioners licensed for the purpose. What is discussed as a social question, then, is inescapably a matter of medical ethics, professional and personal.

Accordingly, in this book the medical chapters are presented first. Practitioners in the disciplines within which the question of euthanasia is most likely to be raised were invited to describe how far their skills and resources enable them to go, given the present state of the medical art and science, before euthanasia becomes a serious issue, a question raised by patients requiring a deliberated response; and then, what that response might be.

The limits of ethical practice are prescribed by law. Chapters on the relevant law in selected jurisdictions follow, including The Netherlands where the relation of law to medical practice is under widespread scrutiny, medical ethics relate to certain principles, developed in philosophy, theology and religion, and to social evolution and technological development. Speculative chapters from these disciplines follow. It will be observed that there is no specific ethics section. The ethics are those of practice, and they are inherent in the descriptions of practice as written by the medical practitioners, themselves the moral agents responsible for their actions. Philosophy, theology, religion and sociology contribute respectively to the ethics of medical decision; they cannot, in themselves, be decisive.

The editors have not expressed a view, or presented a case, either for or against voluntary euthanasia. Neither were contributors to the volume asked to do so. Medical authors were invited to narrate and reflect on professional experience; non-medical authors to widen perspectives from their own disciplines. Readers will form their own judgements and contribute, it is hoped, to present discussion.

The difficult problems that face doctors dealing with terminally ill or severely impaired patients have been discussed in the medical chapters from a variety of areas of clinical practice with different views but with, nevertheless, a surprising degree of consensus. Active termination of life is, in the UK, not only illegal but goes deeply against the grain of medical training and medical ethos. Therefore, though it is clearly recognised that there are indeed situations where the continuation of life is merely a burden to both the patient and to the family, policies for dealing with such situations differ with different clinical backgrounds and with different perceptions of medical duty. There is clearly a widely felt sympathy with A E Clough's ironic, but invariably misinterpreted, couplet 'Thou shalt not kill but needs not strive officiously to keep alive'; although it is equally widely recognised by our contributors that the withholding of treatment does not separate cleanly from active interventions which may shorten life.

It is apparent on comparing the medical with the legal chapters that the views of some societies, as represented by changes in law, have moved apart from (possibly ahead of) the traditional medical view of euthanasia. Despite the social climate of the UK, where there is powerful advocacy for the claims of animals as equal or even sometimes superior to their human counterparts, there is virtually no perceived ethical problem in veterinarians' ending the lives of terminally sick animals, with their owners' consent if not the animals' own; and this practice does not undermine the veterinary role. In human medicine any comparable activity is clearly much more difficult both to justify and to protect from abuse. However, an increasing number of people now use advance directives to indicate their wish not to have their lives prolonged in specified circumstances. This 'negative' form of advance directive, which the Law Commission, the House of Lords' Select Committee on Medical Ethics and the BMA now accept as valid, does not satisfy those who wish to give a 'positive' directive to have their life terminated in similarly specified circumstances – which is currently illegal. It does seem certain that the last words on these matters have not yet been spoken.

This issue of the *British Medical Bulletin* presents a widespread spectrum of views from doctors, lawyers, theologians and social scientists at a time of change and of active debate. The editors hope and believe that the book will be helpful in promoting this debate. The editors are very grateful to all the contributors for agreeing to take part and to Gill Haddock without whose dedication and expert care all their efforts would have come to nought.

Gordon Dunstan
Peter Lachmann
Scientific Editors

Overture: *Quare fremuerunt?*

G R Dunstan

King's College London and Department of Theology, University of Exeter, UK

Why the commotion?

It is hard to realise that the clinical chapters of this book, describing calm, deliberated practice, step by disciplined step as action and outcome are weighed, were written in a world (or half of it) in commotion about euthanasia. The music of Handel haunts the mind: 'why do the nations so furiously rage together; and why do the people imagine a vain thing?' *Quare fremuerunt gentes?*

Evidence of conflict, in Australia, Europe and North America, is inescapable. In February 1995, the Ministry of Health of The Netherlands published a bibliography entitled *Euthanasia and Physician-assisted Suicide in The Netherlands, 1984–1995*[1]; it contains 198 items. The bi-monthly *Journal of Medical Ethics* alone, during the 14 months up to December 1995 while this book has been in preparation, carried 17 relevant articles, letters and reviews. Judicial and Parliamentary activity over roughly the same period are material to the chapters by Brazier and McCall Smith later in this book. The media concentrate attention on the practice of euthanasia in The Netherlands, also described here by Gevers. Only 5 years ago, Europe was in vigorous debate on the Schwartzenberg proposal of 29 April 1991, in the European Parliament[2], on medical assistance for terminal patients. No one who reads can escape the subject.

Is this a new controversy? Pappas, in chapter 18, alleges that euthanasia has been a subject of controversy for thousands of years; but without evidence her assertion lacks probability. Present controversy should not be read back into former practice. Suicide, certainly, has for long been a moral problem: witness Williams in chapter 13 on St Augustine. Assisted suicide, if you like to call it that, has had a long place in soldierly decency on the field of battle. Saul, on the mountains of Gilboa, called on his armour-bearer to spare him from falling wounded into the hands of the Philistines; the man's refusal stemmed, not from any niceties about euthanasia, but from an Israelite dread of laying hands upon the Lord's anointed; an Amalekite had no such scruple[3]. That is one of the world's stories. Tennyson rewrote and embroidered it for Sir Richard Grenville aboard *The Revenge* at Flores in the Azores:

Sink me the ship, Master Gunner – sink her, split her in twain!
Fall into the hands of God, not into the hands of Spain!

Postal address:
Prof G R Dunstan
9 Maryfield Avenue
Pennsylvania
Exeter, Devon
EX4 6JN, UK

And the gunner said 'Ay, ay, but the seamen made reply:
We have children, we have wives,
And the Lord hath spared our lives'.

But the sick bed is not the scene of battle.

It was traditional, accepted because necessary, that some be set aside to die: by the surgeon in battle, the worst wounded; by the midwife at delivery, the unshapely born. It was accepted that some would be helped to die by their doctors, with nothing better to offer. Thomas Percival of Manchester stated, in 1803, the norm of practice in his day, and it was uncontroversial: 'when medicines which are administered to a sick patient with an honest design to produce the alleviation of pain, or cure of his disease, occasion death, that is misadventure in the view of the law, and the physician or surgeon who directed them, is not liable to punishment criminally, though a civil action might formerly lie for neglect or ignorance'[4]. This was the convention behind Lord Devlin's judgement in the case of Bodkin Adams instanced in the chapter by McCall Smith. No doubt the borderline between dose and overdose was even more indeterminate then than now. Practice was matched to capacity, to means at clinical disposal, justified by what is now called the Bolam test, had there been one then. But capacity has increased, as means have been refined, over time. Old expedients inevitably come under scrutiny.

The present controversy, then, is not an ancient one endlessly pursued. 'It has only recently surfaced' as Howarth and Jefferys demonstrate in their chapter; and that for reasons there given. What has been conventional or covert practice is now in open debate. Among other causal factors stand advances in medical skills. Parallel with those advances in pharmacology and neurology which render obsolete the old resort to analgesia by obliteration have come means to prolong life (Searle), even bodily function when personal significance has already departed. (This development in intensive care is to be distinguished from a ruthless determination to persist in futile surgical and other intervention to reverse the course of a disease, regardless of patients' interests: a cast of mind now repudiated in UK medicine.) At the same time, patients have developed a new independence of mind, a refusal of undue dependence. Many wish not to be 'kept alive' beyond a point where it would be better to be allowed to die; some wish to choose the time of their dying, and require doctors to bring about their death. One means of assuring the first is the advance directive, acceptable, apparently, to the law and newly commended to the profession; it is discussed in several chapters of this book (Gevers, McCall Smith, Lemmens, Williams). Those who wish for this to be the means also of the second, that is of euthanasia or of assistance in suicide, are to be disappointed (Brazier): the advance directive can extend no further than the living patient's refusal of consent: it can forbid further intervention; it cannot enjoin any action contrary to lawful medical practice; and direct killing and assistance in suicide are both against the law in Britain.

Some clinicians, it will be observed (Donovan, Dunstan, Roth, Andrews), express caution or scepticism about advance directives; but for reasons stated, not, it must be supposed, from lack of sympathy with their intent. Haworth and Jefferys also express a sociological caution, should the practice spread.

Legal distinctions, clear in themselves, are not always clearly understood. Semantic slippage can occur, even in courts of law. The judgements of the House of Lords and the Court of Appeal, recited by Brazier and McCall Smith, which authorised the withholding or withdrawal of medical treatment, stated explicitly that the law still prohibits active killing: euthanasia is not yet a term applicable to a lawful activity. Nevertheless, a coroner in England, sitting at inquest on a woman who had committed suicide (which, in fact, she had a legal liberty to do), recorded a verdict of 'death by euthanasia' because she had asked for it: she did not want a verdict of suicide. The verdict was welcomed by organisations promoting euthanasia as a 'sign of great progress' towards a desired goal; but the Crown Prosecution Service drew attention to the impropriety[5]. Imprecision of language, deliberate or unwitting, makes for shifty debate and soggy ground for public policy. It was perhaps this which Howarth and Jefferys had in mind in their hint that the media act 'not always over-scrupulously' in engaging with current affairs.

Theologians have not been silent on the social and ethical concerns of the world. Williams and Barnes do not elaborate a case for or against euthanasia in this volume; they were not invited to. Rather, they recall some basic concepts in Christianity and Buddhism respectively – and compassion and reverence for life are common to both – and state their relevance to the debate. Sommerville outlines positions declared by the major Christian Churches in Britain, particularly their virtually unanimous acceptance of the propriety of withholding or withdrawing treatment for valid indications, and their rejection of direct killing. Sommerville mentions also the common acceptance of the 'sanctity of life' principle in the evidence of secular organisations given to the House of Lords' Ethics Committee. Williams, while maintaining fully the conviction which the words express, would be happy to see the words disappear from this discussion. His reason is cogent. The words 'sanctity of life' have become a slogan widely used by groups for whom 'the preservation of life is in all circumstances the overriding imperative in clinical care': a view which is theologically, as well as clinically, untenable. Ethics bedevilled by slogans cannot attend properly to duties.

Clinical practice

This, then, is the context, soberly described, of the euthanasia debate within which medicine is practiced in Britain under the supervision and protection of the law. Practice comes first in this book, and for good reason. Doctors learn from one another: a collection of essays of this sort may help practitioners to keep abreast of one another; and the pointers to palliative medicine in several chapters commend a relatively new specialty. The medical chapters, with one exception, are not written as arguments for or against euthanasia. They describe practice, each doctor's practice, in which he uses skills and resources apt to serve patients' interests in their several conditions, from neonatal to terminal care. Euthanasia occurs as an hypothesis, an option to be considered in circumstances where there is a moral imperative to act (an emotional impulse to act, though hard to exclude, is of itself not enough) when no other effective action seems to be available.

The one exception to this way of writing (Gilbert's) is justifiable in its own right. As other doctors describe their clinical response to patients' needs, so Gilbert describes the organization and distribution of skills throughout a local community to meet needs for palliative, often terminal, care; and in so doing he expresses his conviction that, given such provision, the claims for euthanasia are obsolescent. With consultancies in palliative medicine now established, one escape route to direct killing is closed. It is not enough now for a specialist in one discipline – in rheumatology, perhaps, or some other painful disease – to say 'I can do no more: nothing can be done to ease this pain'. He must first seek another opinion, from one whose specialty is pain control. Only then are the options fully displayed.

In fact, as the Editors note in their Preface, 'there is a surprising degree of consensus' among the doctors writing about the areas of practice in which the issue of euthanasia is most likely to be raised – though more by relatives, it has been reported, than by patients[6]. This unanimity is matched in Sommerville's account in official pronouncements and statements of evidence, published by bodies responsible for the organization, regulation and discipline of the nursing and medical professions. Euthanasia is, on the whole, unnecessary and unwelcome; the future lies with palliative medicine and better terminal care.

There are, however, deviations, hints of dissent. In Sommerville's account, the UKCC, representing nursing organisations, doubted the distinction between acts and omissions. Doubtless they had considered and dismissed weighty philosophical arguments to the contrary; and they have still to reckon with Cartwright's chapter in this book. 'Double effect' seems also to have worried the nurses; but Gilbert doubts whether appeal to double effect is clinically necessary.

Neither have the doctors themselves closed their minds to other views. Donovan admits to strong emotional pressure to comply with a patient's wish to have life terminated; but he holds back from a boundary which should not be crossed. Dunstan, for whom clinical observation is more telling than philosophical speculation, and who finds that euthanasia has little to offer elderly patients, can nevertheless affirm, in words pregnant with enigma, that a patient 'should not suffer for the sake of his doctor's conscience or the law'. (Brazier asks rhetorically, 'why should the suffering patient pay the cost of the law's inadequacy?' But in her conclusion she would seem to prefer Donovan's uncrossable boundary to more policing by the law.) Roth, in his clinical description of the progress of Alzheimer's disease, while stating reasons why doctors should not kill, admits to clinical repugnance to allowing a treatable infection to terminate a patient's life. Andrews is the most explicit of all in his reservations. Given the care of patients in chronic severe disablement, he cannot conceal his repugnance for the expedient of withdrawing nutrition and hydration in order to secure a 'natural death'. In his abstract he goes further in a clear assertion that euthanasia would be a more satisfactory solution.

It would be excessive to read these qualifications to an assumed medical consensus as signs of a professional façade cracking under internal pressures increasingly hard to contain. Rather, they demonstrate how the authors are emphatically not moulding their accounts of clinical management into conformity with a given pattern, an 'official line'. We see here the exercise of clinical decision, that compound of duty with observed fact in a professional and personal relationship transfused with feeling. Within this, boundaries must be under strain. The Editors, expecting this, said they planned no chapter on ethics. The doctors are the responsible moral agents; philosophers and moralists are not.

Why, then, the commotion?

The notion that doctors pursue a bland routine, ignorant of or wilfully blind to the issue of euthanasia, does not fit the facts. Rather, the accounts recall the disciplined calm of a well-ordered intensive care unit in which a team, with pooled knowledge and duties understood, concentrate on the immediate tasks given them by each patient's condition. Doubts may arise from the clinical data; ideological divisions are left for resolution outside.

Ideologies do divide outside. Their impact on the present development of the common law, and on proposed new statute law, is brought out in Brazier's teasing dialectic. Howarth and Jefferys explore their sociological roots, largely, though not entirely, in Europe. Lemmens writes of Americans 'fiercely divided' as polarised ideologies invade courts and legislatures, and frustrate searches for middle-of-the-road expedients like advance directives. (In the UK, advance directives face, so far, a relatively untroubled passage because the common law governing medical practice has excluded direct killing from their ambit *ab initio*.) The US legal pattern is the more complicated by the conflict of two jurisdictions, the Federal and the States', and by the combative forces of religion in a secular state.

Despite many social and economic differences – including different ways of funding health care and litigation – ideology seems to be the chief divider between the UK and the USA in this matter. The USA struggles with an ethics and a constitutional law based on rights; the UK has grounded its ethics and its common law in duties. That vocabulary and culture in the UK are now increasingly infiltrated by 'rights' is undeniable; and that infiltration may yet prove to be detrimental. Where the demand for euthanasia is most clamant, it is voiced in the name of autonomous rights: a 'right to die' is assumed to entail a right to oblige someone else to bring about death. And both Brazier and Lemmens suggest, in their several ways, that the more legislation is invoked to make that enforcement possible, the more law will intrude its unwelcome presence between doctor and patient at the death bed.

Europe too is not without controversy. Gevers's chapter on The Netherlands is exemplary in the literature for its descriptive and analytical treatment of what is often the subject of polemic. Both Howarth and Jefferys and Pappas recognise the Nazi holocaust as an ingredient in the controversy. It is perhaps odd that The Netherlands, which suffered so cruelly under the Nazi occupation, should have pioneered so radical a medical and legal provision. But the memory of the holocaust, a fading force as it may have been in insular Britain until re-awakened by Michael Burleigh's book, *Death and Deliverance*[7], is not forgotten in Germany. In 1989, academic invitations to an Australian philosopher to lecture were withdrawn because of his much-publicised advocacy of euthanasia; and the controversy over academic freedom which followed eclipsed for a time the controversy over euthanasia itself. Fairness of mind may dissuade from exploiting an awful epoch in history in the euthanasia debate; but the propriety of drawing lessons from it cannot be denied.

The book ends, then, not with a solution but with a dissonance to be endured if not resolved. On both sides of the euthanasia debate stands fear. On the one side is alleged a fear of pain; of undue dependence and being, or bearing, a burden; of living too long in a state in which a feeling of worthlessness has stifled proper self-love. On the other side is alleged a fear of doctors: of what even they might do again in a corrupt, tyrannical society; of what they might do now under improper influence, or under pressure from limited resources, if entrusted with the power to end their patients' lives; a fear of the cheapening of life. On these fears, theologians might be expected to have something to say.

References

1 Vlaardingerbroek WFC. *Euthanasia and physician-assisted suicide in The Netherlands.* Rijswijk: Ministry of Health, Welfare and Sport, 1995
2 *Politeia* 7. 22, 1991. 3–38
3 1 Samuel 31:4; 2 Samuel 1:1–16, 17–27
4 Percival T. *Medical Ethics* (1803); Leake CD. ed. Baltimore: Williams and Wilkin 1927. IV vi p. 130. 'Formerly' is perhaps a mistranscription for 'formally'
5 Reported in *The Independent, The Daily Telegraph, Today, The Daily Mirror,* 7 October 1994
6 Editorial. Relatives keener on euthanasia than patients. *BMJ* 1994; 309: 452
7 Burleigh M. *Death and Deliverance. Euthanasia in Germany 1900–1945.* Cambridge: Cambridge University Press, 1994

Decision making in the neonatal intensive care environment

R P A Rivers

Department of Paediatrics, Imperial College School of Medicine at St Mary's London, UK

Consideration as to whether withdrawal of intensive care support might be a more appropriate line of action than to continue with full intensive care has become a part of the life and death decision making process undertaken in neonatal intensive care units. After outlining the moral objectives of delivery of health care, the arguments for taking quality of life and its various components into account during these deliberations are presented. The circumstances in which the appropriateness of continuing care should be considered are highlighted and the care options presented. The crucial importance of allowing time for parents to come to terms with the situation is emphasised as is the need for giving clear guidelines to junior staff over resuscitation issues. Finally, an environment for providing optimal family support during the process of withdrawal is suggested.

Advances in neonatal care are enabling more of the infants who once would have died to be kept alive. This is true for some with severe lung immaturity, with operable congenital malformations and at the extremes of low gestational age. With these advances has also come an improved ability to predict neurologic outcome: appreciation of the predictive significance of the neonatal electroencephalogram, of evoked potentials, of brain imaging[1,2] and of neurologic examination, often enable neonatologists to build up, over days or weeks, a body of information that may strongly predict a life of total incapacity, and sometimes suffering. In such circumstances, it would be an abrogation of one's responsibilities as a doctor to persist with life-maintaining strategies without giving due consideration to whether such management was appropriate.

Much has been written in the past 15 years on the ethical approaches to decision-making in neonatal care. As long ago as 1972, Lorber[3] described criteria for selecting newborns with spina bifida and hydrocephalus for surgical treatment and, in 1973, Duff and Campbell[4] reported the experience at Yale, where 14% of all deaths in the neonatal intensive care unit followed decisions to withdraw treatment. Since then, many have explored the ethical background to discontinuing care[5-7].

The first detailed description of actual experience in a neonatal unit in the UK, where discussions regarding withdrawal of care on 75 infants had been initiated, revealed that a recommendation for withdrawal of

*Postal address:
R P A Rivers, Department
of Paediatrics, Imperial
College School of
Medicine at St Mary's,
Paddington,
London W2 1PGUK*

care was made by the medical team in 51 instances, with parents accepting the decision in 47[8]. Even when parents elected for continuation of intensive care, only 2 of the 4 survived and those had disabilities.

Moral standpoints

If we accept that the moral objectives of those delivering health care can be based on the principles of Beauchamp and Childress[9], and that these may be summarised as the provision of benefits in ways that are minimally harmful, that are fair and just in the distribution of scarce resources, that respect an individual's rights and that provide respect for morally acceptable laws, then we have a framework on the basis of which we may examine the care provision for individual babies and children. As Gillon[10] argues, when treatment is of no benefit in a given situation, then it cannot be regarded as part of the duty of care for the patient, either by doctors or health care workers. The same could be applied to parents and their duty of care for their child.

It follows that life-sustaining treatment should, therefore, not be provided for all infants indiscriminately, but should be used selectively, decisions being based on the diagnosis and prognosis with the future quality of life being an important consideration. The arguments for taking quality of life into account when deliberating over what line of action might serve the infant's best interests as viewed by the infant's advocate (usually the doctor in charge) and by parents, nurses and other health care workers involved, have been debated by Campbell[11]. The importance of quality of life considerations was acknowledged in the report of the *Hastings Center Project on Imperilled Newborns* (1987)[12]. Indeed, courts in the UK have given indication that an infant's future quality of life should have a bearing on medical decision making[13,14]

What is meant by an acceptable quality of life and can the prognosis for an individual ever be so poor that it is morally unacceptable to prolong life? Justification that such a line can be drawn is argued by Doyal and Wilsher[15] and is centred on what is required to justify the possession of human rights. They argue, along the lines of Harris[16], that possession of self awareness is crucial to the claim, as is the ability to formulate aims and to interact with others. That newborns do not possess these attributes, but rather the potential for them, is the basis of their right to respect and life-saving health care. For a given infant, it is only when it becomes clear with certainty that these attributes will never be achieved, that the right to such health care may be called into question. Whilst such arguments are centred firmly on neurologic functioning and the mental attributes that will evolve, consideration has to be given to the possibility of severe suffering – which, paradoxically of course, implies the existence of awareness. Can it be assumed that an anencephalic child is unable to truly 'suffer', the crying behaviour and associated grimaces being of brain stem origin since cortical awareness is lacking? Where cognition remains unaffected, the distress may be great as has been recorded by the high incidence of severe depression with serious spina bifida[17]. The only indication for continuing treatment in an anencephalic infant might be so as to enable the organs to be used for transplantation. Keeping alive for the parents' wishes alone raises the important question: should patients be used for the benefit of others? This subject is returned to later. To paraphrase the view given by Doyal and Wilsher[15]: it is because at birth babies have only the potential for the maturation of cerebral cognition, that the decision to withhold treatment in the face of a predicted awful quality of life does not usually give rise to the feeling that this action infringes the rights of the neonate on behalf of whom it is made. When, through early childhood, more of that potential is achieved, considerations about withdrawal of treatment increasingly relate to the definitions used in adults of brain death or to whether the process of dying is being disproportionately prolonged in a futile situation.

Neonatologists are, however, very aware that the parents will have viewed a growing fetus as an individual, and even as a member of their family, long in advance of birth. This is all the more likely today through the 'sight' they may have had from ultrasound images. Strong bonds are particularly likely to exist where much has been invested in a pregnancy, especially if past pregnancy failures have occurred. Parents and relatives are, therefore, likely to find the notion of withholding, or later of withdrawing care particularly difficult to face, yet they will be the people most concerned for the kind of life that their child may experience[11].

How certain of outcome should one be? Clearly there are going to be occasions when certainty cannot be complete. Several studies have provided indicators that should enable the questions that need to be asked concerning functional outcome, viz communicative abilities, independence as against continuous dependence on medical facilities, the degree of mental or physical suffering and the length of life expectancy[18], to be answered with sufficient certainty. Consideration of these facets of development and future life should provide the health carers and parents with an awareness of the weight of the burden which the envisaged handicap would impose.

The circumstances

In what circumstances should discussions regarding the appropriateness of not initiating medical intervention or of withdrawal of treatment be commenced? I would imagine that neonatologists, unless blinded by the power of technology, are constantly weighing up the evidence presented to them by the obstetrician and family before birth or from the clinical course, investigations and family considerations after birth, whenever a baby is affected by severe malformations, neurologic damage or other very disabling complications. The situations demanding such deliberations have changed little since the publication of Whitelaw's report from the Hammersmith Hospital[8] which detailed the outcome for babies with severe congenital abnormalities, severe acquired neurologic disease and extremely short gestation, then defined as 25 weeks or less. Sauer[19] summarised the report of the Dutch Pediatric Association in which three groups of patients were identified in whom discontinuation of treatment or more active life-ending regimens might be considered. In the first group are those where it is decided that initiation of resuscitation to achieve immediate survival is not considered appropriate on the grounds that the newborn will certainly die regardless of medical (or surgical) intervention or where the prognosis for life is so poor that non-treatment is morally preferable. Such infants will be those with severe multiple congenital abnormalities and the extremely premature, now thought of as less than 23 weeks gestation. In the second group are those dependent on life-sustaining treatment but where death is expected regardless of continuing treatment or where survival, if achieved, is considered to offer virtually no chance of a life that is considered acceptable. Identified in this group would be those with severe intracranial abnormalities – most commonly now seen amongst the very low gestation or severely asphyxiated newborns, but including those with extremely short bowel syndrome or with other severe complications. The Dutch report identifies a third group who, although not directly dependent on intensive care, have a prognosis for future quality of life which is extremely poor. In this group may be found neonates where the withdrawal of care for reasons above does not lead to demise; examples might be babies following severe birth asphyxia who become self-sustaining in the face of extensive brain injury, or those in group one where a decision to withhold initial intensive support or to withdraw maximal support does not result in death but the baby becomes self-sustaining in spite of a very poor outlook; examples might be babies with severe spina bifida and hydrocephalus or infants who would be faced with extreme suffering if they were to survive, such as those with severe chronic lung disease and cor pulmonale.

Options for care

The possible options for care considered in the Dutch report were the continuation or extension of intensive care, the maintenance of the *status quo*, the withdrawal of the most intensive form of treatment, e.g. artificial ventilation whilst continuing routine care, the withdrawal of all life-prolonging measures and, if suffering occurs or is foreseen, the provision of medication to soften or hasten death. Active euthanasia, defined as the giving of drugs with the intention of hastening death, as would occur in the last listed option, remains illegal in The Netherlands, and where death is clearly intended and has therefore to be categorised as unnatural, investigation by the public prosecutor would ensue[20]. This option of management would not be followed by many practising paediatricians there, with preference given to allowing nature to take its course: for example, intercurrent infections would not be actively treated.

Once all treatment is withdrawn, as a consequence of reaching a consensus view with the parents following scrupulous and careful attention to the decision-making process, there remains disagreement as to whether the prolonging of life itself is morally objectionable and administering medication to hasten the inevitable death is morally preferable. Some would regard the continuing of part of life-prolonging treatment as the lesser evil. Nonetheless, continuation in the face of predicted severe outcome, since it may not be in the child's best interests, can be viewed as less than responsible behaviour, with continuation of the provision of respect, warmth and hygiene being the only necessary humane interventions required. This discordance is well expressed by Chiswick[21] when he says that whilst we expect babies to breathe without assistance, all newborns require a carer for nutrition and hydration, and he sees a real moral difference between withholding ventilatory support and withholding fluids and nutrients. Although the moral justification for withdrawal of all life supporting measures has been extensively discussed[10,23], cogent moral arguments put forward by ethicists, even when falling within existing and sometimes tested national legal frameworks, are never likely to replace individual differences in moral outlook which give rise to differing approaches in the management of severely damaged infants.

The difficulty for the doctor in assuming the role of advocate for the baby is that whilst parents may trust their doctor to put their infant's interests first, the provision of outcome information can never be done in a totally non-directed manner which has been asserted as being necessary if excessive paternalism is to be avoided[22]. However, as stressed by Campbell[11], parents expect advice and opinion to be given at times of need and the neonatologist has to balance his or her duties to the infant with those duties owed to the parents rather than leaving the parents to make the decision by themselves. Rather, they must be given ample opportunity to have a voice in the life or death decisions which are finally made by the doctors. Adequate counselling of the parents, together with giving them sufficient time for discussions with their religious and family advisers, if they so choose, is the most crucial part of the decision-making process. Exploration of their wishes and life values will usually allow a consensus to be reached.

Application in practice

When weighing these considerations and applying them in a manner consistent with one's own moral framework and within the law of the country in which one is working, it is vitally important that, at the beginning of life, the junior staff who will be called to emergencies at delivery are given clear directives in regard to resuscitation. They should err on the side of favouring resuscitation unless previous discussions with the parents have resulted in a consensus decision not to initiate resuscitation but to show respect and to provide warmth. Even when a gestation of less than 23 weeks or birthweight of less than 500 g is predicted, there therefore being little chance of intact survival, the gestational age may turn out to be incorrect and, provided there is some indication of life, resuscitation should be offered. Definitions may vary amongst neonatologists as to what constitutes a significant sign of life in such babies; whether respiratory efforts are required or whether even just the presence of the slow heart rate justifies an attempt at resuscitation can be debated. On balance, the baby should be given the benefit of the doubt, although some would regard the withholding of intracardiac drugs if the heart rate does not rise following the establishment of ventilation as sensible, since continued bradycardia would imply serious myocardial and therefore brain hypoxia prior to resuscitative efforts. Clearly, if it proves impossible to resuscitate the baby, death ensues; with survival and arrival in the intensive care unit, continued re-evaluation of the clinical status with acquisition of the parental views will normally enable appropriate decisions to be made. It is important to remember that if born apparently alive, no matter how immature or apparently severely affected, an infant receives full protection of the law and it is no longer acceptable to consign a gasping newborn to the sideroom in the hope that death will follow quickly. As has been previously highlighted[22], apart from the obvious lack of sensitivity in such an action, errors can occur in the calculation of gestational age with a baby surviving damaged as a consequence of imposed hypothermia, hypoxaemia and hypoglycaemia.

Another difficult situation arising at birth is the infant born apparently dead. Since accurate predictions of outcome cannot be made at that moment, full resuscitation should be offered with the decision to withdraw support being left until the response to intervention is observed or until the clinical course and investigational findings over subsequent days provide an indication of the severity of damage. Only by following such an approach can adequate consultation and deliberation be ensured.

However, some very damaged babies will become self-sustaining and, together with their families, will need the full support of available resources, which may not be all that could be desired for raising a very disabled child.

In the preterm infant in whom evidence of severe brain compromise becomes apparent, the morale of the unit can be undermined by the difficult decisions regarding withdrawal that may have to be made after several weeks of providing encouragement to the parents and care for the baby. The strong emotional attachments that staff and parents develop in these situations of high stress must be addressed through and after the decision-making process, and psychological support for the individuals involved should be available. In spite of the establishment of committees to help in the decision-making process in some countries[24], it would appear that British professional and public opinion still prefer that the doctor and parents retain the primary responsibility for withdrawal of care decisions[22,25]. If conflict arises with parents wishing intensive care support to be continued in the face of no long-term positive gain for the infant, then the availability of counselling facilitators may be of value. Although parents have presumptive authority over the welfare of their children, this authority is limited in order to protect the child's best interest[26]. Given time, it must be rare indeed for the authority of the courts to be called upon to take on the role of guardian of the child's interests.

Withdrawal of treatment, and the offering of compassionate support for the distressed parents, are more readily carried out in a location away from the main activity of the unit; the parents, the nurses who are involved, and the doctor in charge are then not distracted by other commitments or demands. For example, it may be possible to continue full intensive care in the parents' bedroom so that they may have some time alone with their infant before the withdrawal phase; in the situation of the single, unsupported mother who may wish to have her own parents present with her, a more private location than the intensive care unit can provide an atmosphere of calm. Provision of relief for the baby from stress or discomfort following withdrawal is part of care for the dying infant and is a humane medical act being in the child's best interests and consistent with our responsibilities to the family and to society[27].

References

1   Volpe JL. *Neurology of the newborn*, 3rd edn. London: Saunders, 1995: pp 348–51
2   Stewart AL, Reynolds EOR, Hope PL *et al*. Probability of neuro-developmental disorders estimated from ultrasound appearance of brains in very preterm infants. *Dev Med Child Neurol* 1987; **29**: 3–11

3   Lorber J. Spina bifida cystica. Results of treatment in 270 consecutive cases with criteria for selection for the future. *Arch Dis Child* 1972; **47**: 854–73

4   Duff RS, Campbell AGM. Moral and ethical dilemmas in the special care nursery. *N Engl J Med* 1973; **289**: 890–4

5   Weir RF. *Selective non-treatment of handicapped newborns: newborn dilemmas in neonatal medicine.* Oxford: Oxford University Press, 1984; pp 143–87

6   Kuhse J and Singer P. *Should the baby live? The problem of handicapped infants.* Oxford: Oxford University Press, 1985

7   McMillan RG, Engelhardt Jr HT, Spicker SF. eds *Euthanasia and the Newborn.* Dordrecht: D Reidel Publishing Co., 1987

8   Whitelaw AGL . Death as an option in neonatal intensive care. *Lancet* 1986; **2**: 328–31

9   Beauchamp TL, Childress JF. *Principles in biomedical ethics.* 3rd edn. Oxford: Oxford University Press, 1989

10 Gillon R. Palliative care ethics: non-provision of artificial nutrition and hydration to terminally ill sedated patients. *J Med Ethics* 1994; **20**: 131–2

11 Campbell AGM. Quality of life as a decision-making criterion 1. In: Goldworth, Silverman, Stevenson, Young, eds. *Ethics and perinatology.* Oxford: Oxford University Press, 1995: pp 104–19

12 Report of the Hastings Center project on imperilled newborns. *Hastings Cent Rep* 1987: **17**: 5–32

13 Brahams D. Medicine and the law: Court of Appeal endorses medical decision to allow baby to die. *Lancet* 1989; **1**: 969–70

14 Brahams D. Life-sustaining treatment for brain-damaged child. *Lancet* 1992; **339**: 1472–3

15 Doyal L, Wilsher D. Towards guidelines for withholding and withdrawal of life prolonging treatment in neonatal medicine. *Arch Dis Child* 1994; **70**: F66–F70

16 Harris J. *The value of life. An introduction to medical ethics.* London: Routledge, 1989: 7–27

17 Dorner S. Adolescents with spina bifida: how they see their situation. *Arch Dis Child* 1976; **51**: 439–44

18 Versluys Z, de Leeuuv R. A Dutch report on the ethics of neonatal care. *J Med Ethics* 1995; **21**: 14–6

19 Sauer PJJ. Ethical decisions in neonatal intensive care units: the Dutch experience. *Pediatrics* 1992; **90**: 729–32

20 Visser HKA. Ethical aspects in paediatrics: clinical care and research. Personal communication, 1994

21 Chiswick ML. Comment on Doyal L, Wilsher D. Towards guidelines for withholding and withdrawal of life prolonging treatment in neonatal medicine. *Arch Dis Child* 1994; **70**: F70

22 Campbell AGM. Ethics at the obstetric–paediatric interface. In: Clements, ed *Safe practice in obstetrics and gynaecology. A medico-legal handbook. Edinburgh, Churchill Livingstone,* 1994: pp 291–303

23 Weir RF. Withholding and withdrawing therapy II. In: Goldworth, Stevenson, Silverman, Young, eds. *Ethics and perinatology.* Oxford: Oxford University Press, 1995: pp 181–2

24 Hoyt JW. Medical futility. *Crit Care Med* 1995; **23**: 621–2

25 Campbell AGM. Quality of life as a decision-making criterion 1. In: Goldworth, Stevenson, Silverman, Young, eds. *Ethics and perinatology.* Oxford: Oxford University Press, 1995: p 91

26 Shelp EE. *Born to die.* New York: Free Press, 1986: Chapter 3

27 Stahlman M. Withholding and withdrawing therapy and actively hastening death 1. In: Goldworth, Stevenson, Silverman, Young, eds. *Ethics and perinatology.* Oxford: Oxford University Press, 1995: pp 165–70

General practitioners and voluntary euthanasia

Christopher F Donovan

North London General Practitioner, UK

Illustrative examples of typical cases met with by a general practitioner on a day-to-day basis.

'It is not death I fear to face, but dying.'
Robert Louis Stephenson

Two general practice situations

'You will help me out, doctor, if things get difficult?' It was a winter's night. Evening surgery was over. I had called on my way home to see how my patient was managing.

Miss A was a highly intelligent 67-year-old spinster. She had asked if I, as her GP, could be as open as possible with her after the diagnosis of cancer had been made. Indeed, the consultant at the local teaching hospital had complained about my telling her that secondaries had spread into her spine and liver. She had asked if she could stay at home until she died. Her niece had moved in to look after her. She was already on an oral mixture of diamorph.

How should a GP respond to her question? I chose to find out what she meant by 'difficult'. 'What would you find impossible?', I asked. 'Excruciating pain. Too much for my niece. Having to go back into hospital' she explained. We discussed these in turn. We agreed to get in extra nursing. As long as her symptoms were controlled, I promised that she could remain at home. (This consultation took place before we had a hospice care team or syringe drivers were available in general practice.) I informed her that the practice nurse would visit in the mornings to see how she was and to give her an injection, and that I or one of my partners would visit at night.

When this discussion was over she repeated her question. 'I'll do all I can', I said. 'What does that mean?' 'It means' I said, 'that if you request it, I will give you an extra large injection of painkillers'. She smiled and relaxed. Then a thought struck her. 'But what if I am unable to speak?' We agreed that she could signal by lifting her right hand in the air and clenching and opening her fist at least twice.

In the event, her pain was well controlled. Her niece and nurses managed wonderfully. No signal was ever given. One night Miss A, after

Postal address:
Dr C F Donovan,
25 Middleway,
London NW11 6SH,
UK

her injection, drifted into sleep and did not wake again. She never asked me if a large dose of painkillers would end her life and I never chose to tell her that it probably would not . . .

Mrs B also lived alone. She was a widow who had two children and grandchildren who regularly visited. When she was told that her secondaries had spread, she joined a voluntary euthanasia society. She brought a copy of their magazine to me, and pointed out the list of ways in which she could end her life. 'Which one would you choose?' she asked. I replied that I would leave it to nature. 'Well', she said, 'I've chosen this one because it only requires 30 tablets. Could you please prescribe'. I told her that I really could not be party to her committing suicide, and she would have to choose a method that did not involve me. 'But' I added, 'I would like to know what would make you feel so terrible, even when ill, that you would end your life'. A host of fears, anger and unhappiness was then expressed.

Once revealed, I and her family could help with these problems. Also a feeling of trust built up between us which stood us in good stead during the weeks ahead.

She did procure her own tablets but she never used them. As the illness proceeded, her attitude seemed to change. With support and effective symptom control she became more peaceful and accepting, and died quietly at home having settled many misunderstandings within her family, listening to her own music.

Discussion

Most of us facing a terminal illness will be anxious and afraid. Part of a GP's task in this situation is to help stop patients building a wall of silence around themselves. If their fears and anger can be shared with both the GP and the family, something can be done to help. As the illness worsens, sharing can continue.

Initially, patients may react by requesting euthanasia. If GPs take this at face value, there is a danger that they can become diverted from the task of helping patients to share their fears, many of which may be based on ignorance as to what may happen as the illness progresses (a request for euthanasia may on the other hand be a way of testing both the GP and the family to see how much support and care is likely to be forthcoming).

If the GP can elicit what lies behind the request and then explain what medicine can offer to help with physical and emotional distress, anxiety can be reduced and acceptance of the inevitable increased. In my experience, as a patient's illness progresses, their perceptions change. Anxiety shifts onto using effectively the time that remains, saying goodbye, and onto the small necessities and enjoyments in life. Few receiving effective palliative care, either at home or in a hospice bed, eventually ask for euthanasia. At the same time, I believe that the double effect of using high doses of diamorph is fully justified to control pain and anxiety where necessary, even if it hastens the end of life.

Active killing – two GP cases

Some readers may complain that the situations described above are not situations in which the GP would be tempted to terminate their patients' lives. I therefore will describe two situations in which I was sorely tempted to do precisely this.

As soon as I delivered Mary at home, I knew that something was seriously wrong. The baby took time to breathe, and was extremely floppy. She was immediately admitted to hospital where a bizarre genetic abnormality with no name was diagnosed. She was sent home to die. Yet she lived for 18 months. I remember visiting in the middle of the night, and sitting with her mother as Mary fought for breath with yet another chest infection. On at least one occasion, her mother burst into tears and shouted, 'when will she die? I can't take any more of this!'

To take the pressure off, I would send the baby back to hospital with a note saying 'Mary has a further respiratory infection which I feel should not be actively treated'. With tipping and fluids, Mary would recover and her mother would wait again for the end. On several visits I was tempted to intervene actively, yet ethical convictions held me back.

Mrs E was a young mother in her forties. She returned home from hospital to be with her husband and two young children for the last weeks of her life. Her secondaries had caused her arms to be virtually paralysed. She lay in a cardiac bed, looking out on her garden, doubly incontinent and unable to do anything for herself. While her GP was away, I visited her. After we got to know each other she said to me one day, 'Please help me to die. Feed me those pills over there. I can't do it myself, and I must get this over'. 'I can't do that' I said, and I found myself apologising to her. When I left that day, I wondered whether I had been treating myself or my patient.

Strictly speaking, the above example of a baby should not come into this contribution for she, like a demented person, is not able to be party to 'voluntary' euthanasia. Yet these two cases illustrate GP situations where the emotional involvement of the doctor is high. The tug to use one's medication to eradicate the distress for both patient and family can become great, to the point of wanting to act to end their lives. In these situations, it is my experience that only a strong ethical belief can maintain a boundary. Should this boundary become broken, GPs, like other doctors, will be faced with many situations where their emotional reaction and subjective values would become the basis on which decisions of life and death would be made.

The GP's relationship with the hospital

Mrs M made me promise that she could return home under my care, and die in her own bed whenever she chose. This promise was made before she agreed to go back into hospital for a further operation for her intestinal obstruction caused by her abdominal cancer. The operation successfully bypassed the obstruction but her general condition deteriorated and it became clear that she was terminally ill.

She asked if she could return home. The ward sister, surgeon and the hospital physician, in fact all the hospital staff told me, her GP, that I would be irresponsible to concede to her request. They argued that it would be impossible in general practice to control her syringe driver, her drip and the riles tube, and that she would probably die before her time in discomfort.

I kept my promise. Mrs M was thrilled to reach her own bed, to be surrounded by her own family and in her own home. She herself removed her riles tube, and we felt it unnecessary to replace it. However, her syringe driver and her drip ran successfully until the end. She was brilliantly nursed by both district and hospice carers and visited two or three times a day by the GP. She died peacefully after a few days, surrounded by her family, the hospice nurse and the family physician.

Discussion

The hospital staff in this situation were sincere in their belief that they could offer Mrs M the best treatment in her last few days of life. However, the GP, knowing that his patient was in her right mind, felt that it was in her interest for him to keep the promise that he had made to her. But the promise was not his only consideration.

One of the differences between GPs and hospital doctors is that GPs who have cared for a family for many years are more likely to know if their patients really mean it when they say they wish to die at home. In addition, the GP knows the environment of the home and how suitable it is for the patient to come home for all the members of the family.

There is another difference; the family physician has more than one patient to consider. Bereavement starts long before the death of a loved one occurs. What takes place during the last weeks and days can have considerable effect on the bereavement process of both adults and children, who need to feel that everything possible was done to help the patient.

In Mrs M's case, it was not just a question of fulfilling the patient's wishes. In one respect the GP chose to back his own judgement and to go against his patient's wishes. Mrs M had arranged for her two children, then aged twelve and ten, to go away when she came home to die. When asked, each of them did not want to go against 'Mummy's wishes', but they both expressed a desire to stay. Their father felt the same. So the GP decided that it was in the interests of the children to share this difficult time with their father and persuaded them to remain and also to attend their mother's funeral.

Advance directives

A living will can be an effective method of opening communication between patients, doctors and their families. It can lead to discussions as to what the patient would like to happen, long before serious illness intervenes. It has proved particularly effective with those suffering from AIDS, and has relieved many who dread being in a vegetative state or unable to communicate as a result of serious illness. Often the GP gets involved, and copies of advance directives tend to be placed in GP patient's records.

Mrs X had a real dread of finding herself seriously ill and being 'officiously kept alive in a hospital bed'. In her forties, she filled in an advance directive and shared it with her family and asked me, her GP, to see that it was enforced. This enabled everyone close to her to know how strongly she felt about ever being in such a situation and it relieved her anxiety.

Ten years later, she got divorced and married a man who lived in The Netherlands. Shortly after this, she rang me from abroad saying she wished to extend her living will to include active euthanasia 'as this was legal in The Netherlands'. 'Would I' she asked 'still be responsible for ensuring that it would be enforced'? I replied that I could not on ethical as well as practical grounds. I urged her to contact a GP in The Netherlands. This she has done, and both she and her close family feel happy about the situation.

The position of Mrs S was very different. She was in poor physical and mental health. She was a 90-year-old widow who had three daughters. who argued amongst themselves. One day I was asked by the youngest daughter to assess her mother and pronounce her in sound mind so that she could sign a new will. Although Mrs S was becoming increasingly forgetful and felt under pressure from her daughter, I concluded that she knew exactly what was going on and declared her 'in sound mind'. A few days later, Mrs S told me that her daughter now wished her to write a 'living will'. 'If you have a second stroke, you could be kept alive in hospital and then possibly put in a home which would be very unpleasant and extremely expensive', her daughter had explained. Mrs S asked me what she should do, adding 'I want to be fair to my daughters. If I ever went into a home and went on living for a long time, there will be no money left for any of them to inherit'. I pointed out that this was not a good reason for signing a living will. I asked her what she felt about being given antibiotics and other medication to keep her alive if she did have another stroke. She replied, 'I would feel bad if I did not do what was best for my daughters'.

So Mrs S signed an advance directive saying she did not wish to be kept alive if she had a further serious illness. Some time later she died of a massive stroke. Signing the living will made her feel that she had done the right thing by her children, and her daughters felt satisfied. Only the GP felt concerned that she had taken this action for questionable reasons.

Discussion

We are all living longer. The cost of medical care of the aged is escalating. Not unnaturally, those who pay, both families and society, will increasingly be tempted to look to euthanasia as a solution to this costly activity.

Advance directives are a wonderful way of sharing a patient's wishes as to what they would like to occur, should they be seriously ill. They also deter keen doctors from overtreating their elderly patients. They have, however, disadvantages. These include the fact that people frequently change their minds when they are ill: advance directives need to be updated; they may not be available at the requisite time; and patients can be put under pressure by both families and society.

Part of the GP's role is to encourage the effective use of advance directives, while diminishing these disadvantages. Publications by the British Medical Association (BMA)[1,2] and Terence Higgins Foundation both describe the advantages and disadvantages of living wills and give examples.

Legally a living will must be observed by doctors insofar as it specifies refusal of treatment; it cannot require a doctor to give treatment which is futile or contrary to clinical judgement, or is unlawful. Even so, the doctor, along with the proxy, need to consider carefully its content and the present position of the patient. It is for this reason important that the GP should discuss exactly what the patient has in mind at the time of writing the living will, and make sure that the document is updated every few years. It is also essential that the GP sees that it is not only attached to the patient's notes, but made available if and when the patient should become seriously ill.

Conclusions

It is impossible to generalise the views of GPs as they vary so much. A review of 100 GPs, in the BMA news review on 8 March 1995, showed that 6 out of 10 family doctors opposed the legislation of 'assisted suicide for the terminally ill patient'. To the question, 'would you, if the law allowed, assist in the suicide of a terminally ill patient if the patient, when mentally competent, has made a witnessed request for euthanasia', 25% said 'yes', 58% said 'no' and 17% said that they 'didn't know'.

GPs' views vary, but their day-to-day life has much in common. I have tried to show in this contribution how GPs are involved in very personal situations with people whom they have known over a long time. GPs also share the fact that they are increasingly short of time.

Thus many GPs are placed in situations where important ethical decisions have to be made in a short space of time. It is here that I believe clear ethical and legal boundaries are necessary. Those who argue in favour of legalising euthanasia inevitably base their case on one or two extreme situations. However once boundaries are removed, the ripple effect will result in the involvement of GPs in a host of less extreme situations and a radically changed GP/patient relationship.

To claim that, in such situations, patients have a right to make the decision as to whether the doctor helps them terminate their lives is, to my mind, to deny the fact that terminal care is a partnership between the physician and the patient, with the family intimately involved. Moreover, patients are not in a position to make sound decisions when they do not know at the start of their illness what is likely to occur. They, therefore, tend to act from fear rather than knowledge. Patients can also, as we have tried to show, be subjected to pressure from their families and society for economic, rather than humanistic, reasons.

The hospice movement and GPs have shown that patients and their families can use their last weeks or days in a productive way. This was the gist of a barrister's summing up in the trial of Dr Carr, accused of attempted murder after injecting a massive dose of phenobarbitone into a patient who had lung cancer. The barrister said, 'however gravely ill a man may be . . . he is entitled in our law to every hour . . . that God has granted him. That hour or hours may be the most precious and important hours of a man's life. There may be business to transact, gifts to be given, forgiveness to be made, a hundred and one bits of unfinished business which have to be concluded.'

Paternalism is in danger of being made into a 'dirty word' and treated as the opposite of respecting patients' right to make their own choices. For GPs to share their training and experiences with their patients, and working with their local hospice, help families make decisions as to how to use their last period of time productively, should in my mind not be dismissed on the grounds of paternalism but be valued as a desirable aim of productive partnership.

Many patients, to their surprise, have found that their last days have brought them quality life, when their symptoms have been well controlled. Moreover, families have been able to look back when grieving with a feeling of satisfaction rather than horror that those last few weeks were used productively. Some patients in this time have created treasured pictures, poems, or recollections which have brought them satisfaction and which have been greatly valued later by their families.

GPs, I believe, should try and achieve these aims rather than concentrating on how and when to end suffering by actively shortening their patients' lives. If this view is taken, then greater emphasis needs to be placed by our profession on learning more of the ever advancing skills of palliative care.

GPs throughout their career need the time to learn to improve communication skills, symptom control (not just pain, but breathlessness, constipation, nausea and psychological distress), and methods of working effectively with their primary and hospice teams.

To run a health service in which doctors who care for terminally ill patients do not have the time and opportunity to keep up to date with such advances is, in my view, ethically questionable.

I applaud symposia like this one which encourage thinking more deeply about terminal care. I feel, however, that we need to encourage these debates early in medical education and to include a deeper consideration of our attitude as doctors to death itself. Like birth, death is a natural process of which we only see one side. If we lived in a culture that accepted death more openly, we, as doctors, might be less apprehensive about the end of life, and, as a result, work more closely with natural forces and not sink into the temptation of fighting them all the way. In addition, it is important for doctors to realise that many people die without medical help, and so avoid the danger of over-medicalising the ending of our lives.

For this reason, I would like to finish with an account of one last GP consultation which made me think deeply about the natural process of dying.

I was woken at 3 a.m. by a 'phone call from a Mrs X. 'Could you come and certify that my husband is dead?' I was shown into an upstairs bedroom and there found Mr X, a 90-year-old patient, lying in his pyjamas on the floor – clearly dead.

Believing that his wife would be distressed, I suggested that we went downstairs. When she had prepared tea and we sat facing each other across the little kitchen table, I told her that I was extremely sorry. 'Don't be sorry' she said. 'It was wonderful!' Surprised, I asked 'what do you mean?' She explained, 'Eric had had a lovely day. He cut the garden hedge, the sun shone, he was feeling fine. As you know he was a Quaker and 'full of peace'. We went to bed early. In the middle of the night he turned the light on and said, 'wake up Edith and join in the party'. He mentioned many of our relatives who were dead and claimed they were in the room having a party. I told him he was dreaming. I wanted to sleep and asked him to turn off the light. This happened twice. The third time I heard a bump. I turned on the light, and found he had fallen out of bed and was as you found him, dead on the floor.' Then she added, 'wasn't it wonderful that all those relatives came to collect him. What better way to go!'

References

1   *Advanced statements about medical treatment. Code of Practice with explanatory notes.* Report of the BMA. London: BMJ Publishing Group, April 1995
2   *Euthanasia.* Report of working party to review BMA guidance. London: BMJ Publishing Group, May 1988

... And a time to die: the medicine of old age

Edmund Dunstan

West Heath and Selly Oak Hospitals, Birmingham, UK

Most deaths in Britain occur in old age, and old people dying have as many symptoms as do the young. Management is complicated by diagnostic difficulty, by the frequency of mental disorder (sometimes treatable) and of severe disability, and by the difficulty in ascertaining patients' feelings.

Decisions about the management of dying are inevitable, and multifactorial, and views of others may be helpful. Cardiopulmonary resuscitation is not indicated if futile, and may or may not be wanted by the patient. Withholding or withdrawing life-prolonging treatment may be justified if the totality of life gained (length and quality) is not justified by the burden of treatment. Decisions are most difficult when the prognosis is poor but not definitely fatal. Palliative care is important, not only in cancer.

Euthanasia is seldom requested at present, and in The Netherlands is carried out less in old people than young. It would do little for the most serious problems of old age.

Death and dying are inevitably an important aspect of the medicine of old age. In 1991, 59% of all deaths in England and Wales occurred in people aged 75 or over[1]. Even an active geriatric service may have a hospital mortality of 15–20%, and a more long-stay unit may well have a higher mortality than this. Especially in more acute settings, many deaths will be sudden, or occur despite appropriate active treatment, but many others will be the end of chronic illness, the management of which may raise other issues. The majority of symptoms are just as common in old people dying as in younger ones, even though outsiders rate them as less severe[2]. There are several features of illness in old age that affect the management of patients with a poor prognosis, and which are much less prominent at younger ages.

Relevant aspects of illness in old age

Diagnostic difficulty

Postal address:
Dr E J Dunstan, Geriatric Department, Selly Oak Hospital, Raddlebarn Road, Selly Oak, Birmingham B29 6JD, UK

Diagnosis may be difficult in the aged. Presentations of serious disease may be non-specific, with falls, confusion or 'just can't cope'. History-taking may be difficult because of cognitive impairment or communication difficulties, and physical and laboratory findings may be confusing in the presence of multiple diseases. The greatest barrier to accurate diagnosis may, however, be lack of time and interest in old people:

geriatricians may miss less disease found at autopsy than other specialists[3]. Plainly the management of a dying patient should start with a diagnosis, though it is true that it is sometimes clearer that someone is dying than why, even after appropriate investigation (which may itself be circumscribed by the patient's condition) has eliminated treatable possibilities. The finding of remediable conditions in patients thought to be beyond help is a common geriatric experience.

Mental disorder

The prevalence of mental disorder in sick old people is of particular relevance to any discussion of euthanasia, such disorder plainly invalidating any request for euthanasia. Mental illness is frequently missed by non-psychiatric medical and nursing staff[4]. Amongst acute geriatric admissions, a prevalence as high as 27% has been reported[4], though others[5,6] have found lower rates of 10–13% for all organic mental impairment, including the important group with delirium, whose mental state is likely to improve with treatment of the underlying physical illness: Bowler *et al.* found this in 5% of their series[4]. Depressive symptoms are also common in elderly in-patients, being found in between 9 and 23%[4-7], though in the majority these symptoms are probably secondary to illness and transient. However, a quarter or more of such patients have a major depressive illness[5-7], which may not be easily diagnosed but requires specific treatment (though how often this is successful in the presence of physical illness is less clear).

Koenig *et al.*[7] noted a correlation between the severity of physical illness and the severity of depressive symptoms. Symptoms of depressive illness, especially anorexia and lethargy, and of physical illness overlap, while some organic conditions, such as giant-cell arteritis, are notorious for presenting as depression. In summary, conditions that affect mental competence or may make elderly people wish they were dead are common and are often treatable – if diagnosed.

Severe disability

A third important feature of medicine in old age is the high prevalence of physical disability. While locomotor causes for this are common, it is neurological disease that usually causes the most severe problems, often with associated mental or communicative disorder (e.g. dysphasia). In addition, many people with dementia eventually become physically disabled as well, whether from the progression of their cerebral atrophy or from a complication such as femoral fracture. Quality of life must therefore often be an issue and, while some severely handicapped old people may be able to tell us about their own quality of life and its implications for their medical management in grave disease, very many cannot. While severe mental disability appears to an observer to be more dehumanizing than its physical counterpart, it is a difficult and skilled task to guess how the sufferer might feel. Though there are now many 'quality of life' scales, I am unaware that any have been validated in populations of multiply handicapped elderly people.

Resources

It may be tempting to the absolutist to ignore the question of resources. However, one patient's use, whether of a ventilator or of a physiotherapist's time, may mean less opportunity for another, unless such resources are in surplus. There is, therefore, an ethical constraint on the use of a resource that would offer another patient a better chance of benefit, and it must be unethical to use it when there is no prospect of doing good. This consideration should not necessarily disadvantage old people: large resources are spent on younger people, for instance with small-cell lung cancer or advanced AIDS, whose prognosis is no better than that of many 85-year-olds. Where there may be a danger that resources may distort judgements is in the provision of long-term care: where this is scarce, may doctors be tempted to prefer death to dependency?

Medical decisions affecting the end of life

Unless we are to attempt to prolong life in any way possible, whatever the cost in iatrogenic suffering and resources (even ignoring any consideration of the quality of the life prolonged), decisions affecting the end of life have to be made. It seems to me that it is the totality of life – so to speak the product of its quality and duration – that doctors should seek to maximize. In most circumstances quality and length will go together: it is where they do not that decisions may become difficult. Quality of life, present and foreseeable, may thus be as important a factor as diagnosis, prognosis and the effects, for good or ill, of possible treatments. It is unlikely that scales for measuring quality of life will ever be either sufficiently validated or discriminating enough to help in the management of individual patients. Mentally clear patients may of course be well able to guide us, but not all will wish autonomy to be thrust upon them, and may wish their doctor to decide for them. At the least, for a doctor to decline to advise is a dereliction of duty. Very often, however, cognitive loss, dysphasia or other communication difficulties make patients' views impossible to ascertain, and their attendants have an inevitable responsibility to decide on management. Except in the case of permanent unconsciousness, I do not believe that we can rely absolutely on previously expressed views, or on advance directives, to predict how people would wish to be treated when they are actually impaired, though such views should certainly not be ignored. Sometimes observed behaviour may tell us something: the dysphagic man with a stroke may show us that the nasogastric tube that feeds him is intolerable by repeatedly pulling it out (though, of course, this action is probably not fully informed). It is important to recognize that 'competence' is not, however convenient it might be for lawyers and philosophers, all-or-none, but a continuum, with moderately impaired patients able to make choices on some matters but not on others. Relatives' opinions may be useful, though it has been found that many old people would not wish their relatives to be involved in resuscitation decisions[9], and it is certainly wise to stress that decisions on medical management are the doctor's not the relatives'. The views of other professional staff, especially nurses, in frequent and close contact with the patient are often most valuable. Although 'substituted judgement' (i.e. what the patient would be thought to wish if still competent) has been said to be the preferred approach[9], in reality deciding what is best for this patient now must be a far more complex process.

Cardiopulmonary resuscitation

The decision affecting the end of life taken most often is whether or not someone should be subjected to cardiopulmonary resuscitation, a much misunderstood procedure. It is effective only against a tiny part of the differential diagnosis of death – principally ventricular fibrillation in acute heart disease. To withhold it from patients in whom it has even less chance than usual of success is not neglect, therefore, but good medicine. A wide variety of prognostic factors in the success of resuscitation have been described (for review, see[10]), but in general other significant illness diminishes the chance of success. This presumably accounts for the poorer outcome in housebound and older patients. Dementia and stroke also may carry a poor prognosis. Though knowledge about resuscitation is often poor[11,12] a substantial but variable proportion of elderly in-patients would wish to be revived[11-13], possibly more in the acute stage of illness than before discharge[13], but probably fewer women than men[11,14].

Patients are less likely to favour resuscitating disabled, and particularly mentally disabled, old people[8,11–13] though we cannot assume that those studied are necessarily good proxies. In most studies, patients have wished to be involved in decisions on resuscitation, but not all wish relatives to be involved[8], and patients' and their doctors' views correlate poorly[8,13,14]. My own practice is now to consider whether there is a worthwhile chance of resuscitation succeeding, and if so to ask the patient if it would be desired. As dementia is a grave progressive disease affecting the ability to decide, I doubt whether offering resuscitation is a kindness.

Withholding or withdrawing specific treatment

Decisions about stopping, or not starting, specific treatment also have to be made frequently. In The Netherlands, such decisions have been estimated to be involved in 17.5% of all deaths (and more in old people)[15]. The justification for such decisions should be that the burden of either the treatment or of the disability and distress in the life prolonged would give less of a life than a conservative 'wait and see' or palliative policy. A conservative or palliative line is more clearly justified when the underlying prognosis is clearly grim, as in advanced cancer or in the last stages of dementia. There is a more difficult judgement to be made when the underlying condition is severe but chronic and stable (such as a severely handicapping stroke of long standing), and a more difficult one still when the prognosis is undoubtedly poor, but not certain. The subtype of stroke described as Total Anterior Cerebral Infarction illustrates this group: by one year, 60% of those affected are dead, and only 4% are independent[16] – not that an independent life is the only life worth living. Many such patients will need artificial hydration to survive – but survival is likely to be in a severely handicapped state, and is in any case less likely if dysphagia is present[17]. I now hydrate if the patient is conscious, to avoid the symptom of thirst, but, as the prognosis is so much worse with a depressed conscious level, feel that it is reasonable not to do so if the patient is comatose, as suffering is unlikely. Plainly, withholding or withdrawing active treatment entails the obligation to provide palliation for symptoms ('Keep comfortable, wait and see.'), but there may be a gradation of responses. Thus, active specific treatment of acute pulmonary oedema or a fractured femoral neck may be the most expeditious way out of suffering. In other circumstances limited treatment, such as blood transfusion up to a limit, but not invasive measures such as laparotomy for gastrointestinal bleeding, would seem to be the right balance. I sometimes use what I think of as the dog test to help me decide how invasive I should be with a patient who cannot understand or consent: though 'I wouldn't do it to a dog' usually has a derogatory tone, most owners are fond of their animals and desire their welfare. By analogy, would I impose the discomforts and hazards of a particular treatment on a patient who could not make sense of it? It is worth emphasizing that a conservative line is not a death-sentence, as patients often recover despite, or perhaps because of, the stopping of specific treatment. Leaving the outcome to the patient's own powers (or, to some, the will of God) may be an appropriate acceptance of biological determinism. This is illustrated by a notable study of the effect of antibiotic treatment of fever in patients with Alzheimer's disease[18]: the more advanced the dementia, the less difference did antibiotics make to survival. Finally, I have often found an aphorism of Dr D A F McGill useful: 'we are not here to perpetuate misery' – treatment with that effect is an abuse of medicine.

Palliation

Palliative care, where death is inevitable, is an indispensable part of humane geriatrics, and needed in a much wider spectrum of conditions than malignant disease, in which as a specialty it has developed. Its ethics are discussed elsewhere in this volume.

Euthanasia in old age

Not surprisingly in view of its universal illegality, published clinical experience of euthanasia (as distinct from philosophical debate, arguments from one side or the other, or opinion surveys) is scanty or anecdotal. My own experience is that patients ask me about it perhaps once or twice a year, and not all of those are in fact dying. This number would be equivalent to less than 2% of all those dying under my care. Though sometimes such requests are a response to short-term distress, or do not really mean what they say, many arise from severe distress that must be recognized and ought not to be brushed aside, though I do not find a suitable reply easy to find. When a more general reference to wishing to die is made, the possibility of a depressive illness must be borne in mind. There are a number of often very old people without any other evidence of depressive illness who feel quite rationally that they have run their course and are ready to die (but are not necessarily asking to be killed). A patient asking for euthanasia should certainly have symptoms controlled as aggressively as necessary, and should not suffer for the sake of his doctor's conscience or the law.

The Dutch experience

The Dutch experience[15] gives some information on euthanasia in old people. It accounts for a smaller proportion of deaths in old people than at all ages. Possible reasons for this include older people being less likely to ask, out of tradition, more often being female and less often dying of cancer (male sex and malignant disease both being associated with euthanasia), and more likely to die in nursing homes.

In The Netherlands, nursing home physicians are less likely to practice euthanasia than general practitioners. This might be because of different attitudes or expectations, or better palliative care skills. Old people are more likely to have a mental infirmity that would invalidate a request. It is notable that fear of dependency was a factor in 35% of requests at all ages. This might affect old people particularly, and it would be of concern if they felt they should be killed really for others' sake.

Bliss[19] has argued, on socioanthropological grounds, that families should have an important role in decisions about euthanasia for dependent elderly relatives. The proportion of elderly people who would not wish relatives to be involved in resuscitation decisions would clearly argue against such a practice, even if euthanasia at patients' own request were accepted (which must surely be the limit of discussion). It is even rarer for relatives to ask me for euthanasia than patients.

It is often argued that there is no real difference between euthanasia and withholding or withdrawing life-prolonging treatment. There is, however, a clear subjective difference to the doctor involved, which cannot be entirely ignored. The actual cause of death is different – drug rather than disease. Most importantly, non-treatment allows survival if this would be the natural course of events while euthanasia eliminates this possibility.

Conclusion

The management of dying in old age is complicated by mental infirmity, considerations of quality of life in severe disability and difficulties in establishing what many patients would wish for themselves. Previously expressed views, views of relatives and the opinion of colleagues in other disciplines may help the doctor in his responsibility of deciding what is in the patient's interest. There are a spectrum of lines of management that should allow death at the most suitable time and with the minimum of suffering, and which should obviate two commonly expressed reasons for euthanasia – fear of intolerable pain and fear of burdensome medical interference, though fear of dependency must remain. There are plausible reasons why euthanasia, where tolerated, is less used in old people. Voluntary euthanasia has little to offer to sufferers from the most devastating problems of old age, which are associated with loss of mental competence and are predominantly chronic rather than terminal.

References

1 Office of Population Censuses and Surveys. *Mortality Statistics, General.* London: HMSO, 1993: pp. 2–3

2 Cartwright A. Dying when you're old. *Age Ageing* 1993; **22**: 425–30

3 Puxty JAH, Horan MA, Fox RA. Necropsies in the elderly. *Lancet* 1983; i: 1262–4

4 Bowler C, Boyle A, Branford M, Cooper SA, Harper R, Lindsay J. Detection of psychiatric disorders in elderly medical in-patients. *Age Ageing* 1994; **23**: 307–11

5 Burns WK, Davies KN, McKenzie FR, Brothwell JA, Wattis JP. Prevalence of psychiatric illness in acute geriatric admissions. *Int J Geriatr Psychiatry* 1993; 8:171–4

6 Cooper B. Psychiatric disorders among elderly patients admitted to hospital medical wards. *J R Soc Med* 1987; **80**: 13–6

7 Koenig HG, Meadow KG, Cohen HJ, Blazer DG. Depression in elderly hospitalized patients with medical illness. *Arch Intern Med* 1988; **148**: 1929–36

8 Morgan R, King D, Prajapat C, Rowe J. Views of elderly patients and their relatives on cardiopulmonary resuscitation. *BMJ* 1994; **308**: 1677–8

9 Fletcher JC, Spencer EM. Incompetent patient on the slippery slope. *Lancet* 1995; **345**: 271

10 Dautzenberg PLJ, Broekman TCJ, Hooyer C, Schonwetter RS, Duursma SA. Patient-related predictors of cardiopulmonary resuscitation of hospitalized patients. *Age Ageing* 1993; **22**: 464–75

11 Gunasakera NPR, Tiller DJ, Clements LTS-J, Bhattacharya BK. Elderly patients' views on cardiopulmonary resuscitation. *Age Ageing* 1986; **15** 364–8

12 Liddle J, Gilleard C, Neil A. The views of elderly patients and their relatives on cardiopulmonary resuscitation. *J R Coll Physicians Lond* 1994; **28**: 228–9

13 Potter JM, Steward D, Duncan G. Living wills: would sick people change their minds? *Postgrad Med J* 1994; **70**: 818–20

14 Hill ME, MacQuillian G, Forsyth M, Heath DA. Cardiopulmonary resuscitation – who makes the decision? *BMJ* 1994; **308**: 1671

15 van der Maas PJ, van Delden JJM, Pijnenborg L, Looman CWN. Euthanasia and other medical decisions concerning the end of life. *Lancet* 1991; **338**: 669–74

16 Bamford J, Sandercock P, Dennis M, Burn J, Warlow C. Classification and natural history of clinically identifiable subtypes of cerebral infarction. *Lancet* 1991; **337**: 1521–6

17 Gordon C, Langton Hewer R, Wade DT. Dysphagia in acute stroke. *BMJ* 1987; **295**: 411–4

18 Fabiszewski KJ, Volicer B, Volicer L. Effect of antibiotic treatment on outcome of fevers in institutionalized Alzheimer patients. *JAMA* 1990; **263**: 3168–72

19 Bliss MR. Resources, the family and voluntary euthanasia. *Br J Gen Pract* 1990; **40**: 117–22

Euthanasia and related ethical issues in dementias of later life with special reference to Alzheimer's disease

Martin Roth

Trinity College and the Clinical School, University of Cambridge, Cambridge, UK

Increased public interest and concern regarding euthanasia have been aroused in recent years by a number of developments. A succession of judgments pronounced by Courts of Law in different parts of the world have, in recent years, sanctioned the withdrawal of life sustaining procedures in cases of prolonged and irreversible unconsciousness and in patients suffering from painful and distressing terminal diseases. They have, therefore, pronounced euthanasia in these circumstances to be legally and ethically justified. This has generated wide ranging debate regarding the ethics of management of those judged beyond hope of recovery or improvement and near the terminal phase of their lives. The practice of euthanasia in The Netherlands, which has been in progress for a number of years, has also served to focus the attention of the medical and legal professions, and the public at large, upon the ethical, legal and clinical aspects of euthanasia. In the majority of patients, life had been terminated on request. But in a substantial minority, it had been undertaken on an involuntary basis. The scale of the practice of euthanasia in The Netherlands in recent years has yielded a vast body of information regarding the moral and practical dilemmas posed for doctors, families and society concerning patients who are chronically unconscious and ambiguously poised between life and death. As a high proportion of those whose lives were terminated were of advanced age, the lessons learned are closely relevant for the specific theme of this paper.

Euthanasia in The Netherlands

Postal address:
Professor Sir Martin Roth,
Trinity College,
Trinity Lane,
Cambridge CB2 1TQ UK

In 1993, the Dutch Parliament introduced legislation for the legal regulation of euthanasia. This had followed from analysis of the results of an investigation into life terminating actions in health care commissioned by the Attorney General of the Supreme Court. The findings of the enquiries and the effects of the new legislation have been reviewed in a recent ethical critique of the new law[1]. Jochemsen reported that, of the 129,000 deaths from all causes in The Netherlands in 1990, euthanasia had been applied in 2,300 persons out of 9,000 who had requested it. 400 persons had been assisted to commit suicide and, in 1,000, euthanasia had been applied without a specific request. In a further 22,500 persons, death had followed treatment for intensified pain or other symptoms either with the explicit purpose of shortening life or without taking into account the likelihood that this might prove to be a consequence of such treatment.

Some authorities have judged these developments as progress towards the humane practice of euthanasia. Jochemsen was critical and his conclusion, after a painstaking review, was that once official toleration or approval was given to the practice of life termination, it 'develops a dynamic of its own that resists effective controls'. He judged the new legislation as protecting life no more and very probably less, effectively than did the old. It is evident from Jochemsen's report that practice of euthanasia has escalated since the introduction of the new legislation. As the cause of death is stated in the death certificate as the original illness rather than euthanasia, the deliberate termination of the patient's life is not declared. It is not, therefore, subject to legal supervision or review. The Minister of Justice has, however, recently announced that 'as a general rule' doctors reporting a case in which they have ended the life of a patient without his explicit request will have to face prosecution[2].

Implications for Alzheimer's disease

These are challenging and disturbing facts. They are of particular concern for those psychiatrists and physicians who are engaged in the care of patients with Alzheimer's disease and a number of other less common forms of dementia in late life. There are some 600,000 persons in the UK suffering from Alzheimer's disease and approximately two-thirds of these patients spend the last 1–3 years of their lives or longer in chronic wards of psychiatric or general hospitals, or nursing and residential homes. They are in a progressively insensate state. It is one of the supreme ironies of this branch of medical practice that many patients with depressive illness in late life have compelling suicidal ideas and some carry them into effect. Yet, if the condition had been treated, the underlying depressive illness would have probably been brought under control along with the suicidal urges it had caused. 'While there is depression there is hope.' In contrast, those with advanced Alzheimer's disease virtually never attempt suicide or ask to be put to death despite the intractable character of the disorder and the state of humiliating helplessness it causes. And there is no treatment that will cure or arrest the progress of this disease. Among those with advanced Alzheimer's disease, it is relatively common practice to omit resuscitation when coma supervenes as the result of acute respiratory or other infection, stroke or cardiac failure. And, in some cases with advanced dementia, treatment for some complicating disease is withheld even though the patient remains conscious. But such practices are inconsistent and rarely recorded accurately or at all. No criteria have been set down to define, in a manner as precise and reliable as possible, the clinical features of the declining 'insensate' phase of Alzheimer and other forms of dementias. Nor have the moral and legal issues posed by management been evaluated so as to ensure that such practices can be kept within ethically acceptable limits.

The chronically unconscious condition, known as the 'persistent vegetative state (PVS)' is irreversible in most cases after a duration of 6–12 months. Alzheimer's disease differs in two significant respects. During the greater part of its course, no kind of vegetative state is present. A vegetative state of a different character is manifest in the final 1–2 years or a period of a few months. The Judgements pronounced regarding PVS have provided valuable guidance for approaches to the ethical issues posed by vegetative states. But their clarity owed something to the relatively unambiguous and categorical nature of the issues in the case of PVS. Secondly, whereas PVS is a condition of extreme rarity, Alzheimer's disease is a common condition in old age with a prevalence of 10% among those aged 75 years and over and 20% among those aged 85 years and over[3]. It represents a major medical, social, ethical and political problem in the contemporary world. This cannot be said of PVS. Yet this is the only disorder in which the many ambiguities and conflicting views have been submitted to a searching analysis followed by authoritative judgements in Courts of Law regarding the ethical and legal justification of suspending life-supporting measures.

The clinical profile in the first few years of the mental deterioration in Alzheimer's disease differs in significant respects from the features of PVS. But there is sufficient in common between the final insensate phase of Alzheimer's disease and PVS for the knowledge gained and the judgements expressed about PVS to help resolve the current uncertainties and moral enigmas posed by the more complex vegetative syndrome in which the lives of those with the Alzheimer syndrome terminate. The clinical features of the PVS and the judgements in the courts of the UK regarding the therapeutic and ethical problems at present will, therefore, be reviewed first in the sections that follow.

The persistent vegetative state

The syndrome was first described as a sequel of brain damage by Jennet and Plum[4]. Patients in a PVS appear to be awake, but exhibit no sign of normal conscious awareness. Although their eyes are open, they respond neither to visual, auditory or tactile stimuli. They make vague sounds, but are incapable of speech or understanding, and cannot respond to communication. Respiration is unaffected, although artificial respiration may be required at intervals in some cases; eye movements are preserved, swallowing reflexes are intact and a sleep/wake cycle is maintained. They have, however, to be fed by a nasogastric tube, the bladder has to be evacuated by an indwelling catheter and the bowels by enema. Intermittent urinary infection is invariable and requires treatment with antibiotics. Although there is extensive destruction of the neocortex, the criteria for brain stem death are not satisfied. Moreover, to his relatives, the patient appears alive with his eyes open and in some movement. His breathing appears most of the time to be spontaneous and effortless, but help with artificial ventilation may be intermittently required. They are incapable of voluntary movement and can feel no pain. Although seemingly awake with eyes open, they do not perceive their surroundings and, like comatose patients, they make no response to stimuli. Those with PVS do not suffer only from the total loss of their cognitive functions. Their ability to feel or express emotions is destroyed; they neither smile nor shed tears nor show signs of anger or hostility. The presence of residual emotional faculties would have enabled them to emit some primitive signals or communications to others. There is no recognisable vestige of their erstwhile features of personality manifest. The patients appear alive, awake, breathing normally, and a brief involuntary movement may be interpreted as a response to a question. Hence, relatives initially find it difficult to understand the seriousness of their condition.

There is evidence from postmortem studies that patients with PVS in whom the condition has persisted for months or years have suffered extensive damage to the cerebral neocortex. The brain stem is, however, intact and vegetative reflexes such as breathing, swallowing and cough and gagging reflexes are maintained.

After 3 months of unconsciousness in PVSs not caused by trauma, recovery, usually with severe residual disablement occurred only in 7% of cases. After 6 months in a PVS there were no recoveries[5,6]. The Medical Ethics Committee of the British Medical Association[7] has stressed the imperative need for early medical treatment and nursing care, courses of intensive stimulation and the provision of appropriate nutrition, as offering the best hope of the partial recovery that may follow in a proportion, usually with residual cognitive deficit.

It will be evident that the cerebral functional systems, that had mediated their cognitive skills, emotional responsiveness and their individual traits of personality, cannot have been totally destroyed from the outset in all cases. For, in the first few months, they can be re-activated with the aid of an intensive programme of stimulation, feeding and repeated arousal. This course of events ensued in the celebrated case of an 86-year-old lady, Carrie Coons[8]. It was subsequently argued that she may not have been a typical case. But this is not strictly relevant.

Some other chronic syndromes of chronic helplessness

In the course of a number of the hearings, passing reference was made to other rare conditions that pose problems similar, in certain respects, to those of the PVS. They include the 'locked in' syndrome due to a haemorrhage in the pontine part of the brain stem, which deprives patients of all voluntary motor control except for movements of the eyelids and vertical gaze. But they do not suffer from unconsciousness or cognitive failure. They are awake and vigilant, though able to communicate only through their eye movements; there is total paralysis of their other muscles. Such patients present fundamentally different and particularly difficult ethical problems in that they are able, albeit with difficulty, to express their wishes about their fate. Their basic personality must, therefore, be relatively intact. Another rare phenomenon mentioned was an advanced case of Guillain-Barré syndrome in which there was total paralysis, but no mental impairment. Yet termination of life had been sanctioned on the strength of the request made by the patient, who was unable to endure his totally helpless state. It would have to be established, as far as possible, that such a person was not passing through a transient state of despair through depression before acceding to such a request.

Judgement regarding therapeutic, ethical and legal aspects of PVS

On 9 December 1992, the Court of Appeal in England[9] considered an appeal against a judgment that had been made in the Family Division of the High Court[10] in the case of Anthony Bland, who had sustained crush injuries of his lungs in the Hillsborough Stadium disaster. As a result, he suffered cerebral anoxaemia which caused irreversible damage to the cerebral cortex of his brain and left him in a PVS from which he had shown no sign of arousal over a period of three and a half years. It was ruled in the High Court, in a judgment delivered by the President, Sir Stephen Brown, that it was permissible for the medical staff in charge of the patient Anthony Bland to discontinue procedures that had been required to preserve his life. In these terms Sir Stephen was granting the declaration sought by the Health Authority responsible for the hospital where the patient was receiving treatment.

The case was referred to the Court of Appeal (Bingham, Butler-Sloss and Hoffman) which ruled that the medical staff caring for the patient would be judged as acting within the law if they discontinued life sustaining measures from Anthony Bland. Artificial hydration and nutrition were assumed in this judgment as constituting medical treatment. There had been unanimity among the medical authorities regarding the diagnosis of PVS and in respect of the opinion that there was no hope of recovery or of improvement in his condition. Treatment would have been of no benefit to the patient and the principle of the sanctity of life was not, therefore, violated by its cessation. On the other hand, the invasive manipulation of his body involved in life support actions, for a patient who had been in PVS for more than 3 years, was not to be regarded as a duty; doctors were not entitled to continue it, since the patient could not have any further interest in the prolongation of what was a mere existence rather than a life in any real sense. The intrusive measures employed constituted a violation of his dignity and the integrity of a human being and his right to a peaceful death.

The decision of the Court of Appeal was upheld in the House of Lords[11] (Kintel, Goff, Lowry, Browne-Wilkinson and Mustill) to which it had been referred in a final appeal. The contributions made by the Judges in the Court and the House of Lords constitute one of the most comprehensive evaluations of the ethical, philosophical and legal aspects of those who have been permanently deprived of their higher mental faculties and are in a chronic and intractable state of unconsciousness.

It is worth quoting one passage from a judgment in the Appeal Court hearings in full, in that it set out, with particular clarity, the main principles that require consideration when decisions are being formed regarding the justifiability of suspending life sustaining treatment in chronic states of unconsciousness. The statement of Lord Justice Hoffman was in close accordance with that made by the other Judges in the Court. Its particular relevance in the present context resides in its intellectual and moral authority and the clarity with which he discriminated between forms of management of those trapped in a state of incurable mental oblivion, which are ethically and legally valid, and those which are invalid, because they violate the principle of sanctity of human life.

In my view, the choice which the law makes must reassure people that the courts do have full respect for life, but that they do not pursue the principle to the point at which it has become almost empty of any real content and when it involves the sacrifice of other important values such as human dignity and freedom of choice. I think that such reassurances can be provided by a decision, properly explained, to allow Anthony Bland to die. It does not involve, as counsel for the

Official Solicitor suggested, a decision that he may die because the court thinks that his 'life is not worth living'. There is no question of his life being worth living or not worth living because the stark reality is that Anthony Bland is not living a life at all. None of the things that one says about the way people live their lives – well or ill, with courage or fortitude, happily or sadly – have any meaning in relation to him. This in my view represents a difference in kind from the case of the conscious but severely handicapped person. It is absurd to conjure up the spectre of eugenics as a reason against the decision in this case.

Thus in principle I think it would be right to allow Anthony Bland to die. Is this answer affected by the proposed manner of his death? Some might say that as he is going to die, it does not matter how, Why wait for him to expire for lack of food or be carried off by an untreated infection? Would it not be more humane simply to give him a lethal injection? No one in this case is suggesting that Anthony Bland should be given a lethal injection. But there is concern about ceasing to supply food as against, for example, ceasing to treat an infection with antibiotics. Is there any real distinction? In order to come to terms with our intuitive feelings about whether there is a distinction, I must start by considering why most of us would be appalled if he was given a lethal injection. It is, I think, connected with our view that the sanctity of life entails its inviolability by an outsider. Subject to exceptions like self-defence, human life is inviolate even if the person in question has consented to its violation. That is why although suicide is not a crime, assisting someone to commit suicide is. It follows that, even if we think Anthony Bland would have consented, we would not be entitled to end his life by a lethal injection.

On the other hand, we recognise that, one way or another, life must come to an end. We do not impose on outsiders an unqualified duty to do everything possible to prolong life as long as possible. I think that the principle of inviolability explains why, although we accept that in certain cases it is right to allow a person to die (and the debate so far has been over whether this is such a case) we hold without qualification that no one may introduce an external agency with the intention of causing death. I do not think that the distinction turns upon whether what is done is an act or omission. The distinction is between an act or omission which allows an existing cause to operate and the introduction of an external agency of death.

To evaluate the relevance of the judgements pronounced regarding PVS for the most highly prevalent form of dementia, namely Alzheimer's disease, requires a preliminary review of the diagnosis, course and the features of the form of vegetative state in which the disease terminates in most patients.

The clinical features, course and complications of Alzheimer's disease

Diagnosis of Alzheimer's disease

The first and foremost clinical and ethical duty of the psychiatrist or physician is to exclude the possibility that he is dealing with manifestations of normal ageing or with some relatively benign and treatable condition rather than the illness most dreaded by elderly persons.

Many of those in the seventh or later decades of life begin to experience some impairment of memory. The deficits that accompany normal senescence are mild, inconsistent, circumscribed and non-disabling. The skills required for negotiating the tasks of everyday life are largely intact, emotional life is preserved and deterioration does not follow.

Depressive illness with the slowing of thought and movement and the loss of self-esteem and confidence it engenders has to be considered and the increased risk of suicide, in men in particular, born in mind. Appropriate treatment abolishes or relieves the symptoms in most cases.

A wide range of metabolic and other physical diseases may mimic primary dementias, such as Alzheimer's disease. Tumours of the frontal or temporal lobes, chronic subdural haematoma, myxoedema and vitamin B_{12} deficiency can cause progressive mental deterioration with cognitive impairment as the main feature, although emotional characteristics and the personality are better preserved in the secondary dementias than in Alzheimer's disease. Sub-acute bacterial endocarditis has, in recent years, become more often manifest in old age and middle life. Dementia may develop as a non-metastatic complication of bronchial or other carcinoma but the primary condition sometimes remains occult. A dementia-like illness may develop in association with the 'atypical hyperthyroidism' of elderly persons and during long courses of treatment with steroids. A high standard of clinical vigilance and care is essential, since the symptoms of many forms of physical illness are relatively 'silent' in the aged with fewer conspicuous symptoms than in the young. Yet only in those diagnosed and treated at an early stage is there hope of reversing or arresting the progress of mental deterioration.

Stages in the progression of Alzheimer's disease

During the greater part of the course of Alzheimer's disease, which may endure for 7–8 years and more in some cases, there is no sign of coma or of a PVS unless some complications, such as a stroke (in 'mixed' cases), a head injury following a fall, or a severe infection (such as pneumonia or septicaemia), supervenes as an additional complication. Otherwise, comatose or PVSs occur only in the final 1–2 years or few months.

In the first stage of about 2 years, symptoms comprise impairment of memory, decline of interest and a gradual diminution of capacity for reasoning, calculation and abstract thought.

In the second stage of 3–4 years, progressive intellectual impairment, personality deterioration and lability of the emotions, followed by blunting and apathy, occur. Focal psychological deficits combine to present more clear evidence of an advancing degeneration of the cerebral cortex. Impairment of language is reflected by increasing difficulty in naming objects and finding words. During the later parts of this stage, there is increased loosening in the cohesion of language and difficulty in the expression and comprehension of speech. Growing impoverishment and impediment in writing and reading reflect progressive demolition of the regions in the brain concerned with storage, integration, and creative use of language. Apraxia renders the patient dependent on others for dressing and bathing and he becomes incapable of feeding himself or responding to requests or commands. Agnosia adds to confusion and incompetence in daily living. Mood disturbance, usually a depressive disorder associated with retardation or agitation, may become manifest at this stage in many patients in this phase of the illness or earlier.

A proportion of those affected are aware of the decline in their mental faculties and, fearing a mindless state, ask for their lives to be brought to an end. There is rarely, if ever, any medical or ethical justification for responding to such requests and deliberate termination of life is unjustified and illegal. The self-destructive ideas emanate in many such patients from a depressive disorder and the symptoms usually respond to treatment drugs and psychotherapy, often with some improvement in cognitive deficits.

Towards the end of this phase, there are disturbances of posture and gait, an increase in muscle tone and, in about 25% of patients, a delusional hallucinatory psychosis with a fluctuating course makes its appearance. Delusions are mainly concerned with dispossession, displacement and persecution and generally respond to treatment with neuroleptic drugs.

A sudden steep decline of consciousness with mental confusion, incoherence of speech, unresponsiveness and sudden onset of incontinence may be due to acute clouding of consciousness or delirium. This always has a specific physical cause, such as pneumonia, gastrointestinal infection with dehydration, or transient cerebral ischaemia. Many such complications respond to treatment and the symptoms of ischaemic episodes usually resolve without residual disablement. The individual remains recognisable as the person he was in a substantial proportion of patients and some retain a limited and variable ability for verbal and emotional communication with others.

But, in the early and middle stages of the disease, the ethical, medical and psychological problems posed for those responsible for the care of the patients are more, paradoxical and difficult to resolve than they proved in the PVS. A limited range of intellectual functions remains. There may be disorientation, memory is severely impaired and speech incoherent. But for brief spells at a time, the patient shows signs of comprehension and recognition of the identity of husband or children and friends is manifest. Facial expression breaks through the mask of apathy and unfolds towards a smile and then the eyes fill with tears. Something of life with features characteristic of the manner in which the person lived remain. In a frail, enfeebled state and, as judged by the rate of progress of the dementia, only 2 or 3 years of life remain. But, for some relatives, the continued life of a loved mother or father or spouse in this state is deemed precious. Death is for them an enemy to be defeated until all individual traces of personality and mental life have been expunged. Their feelings have to be treated with respect and consideration.

No categorical imperatives can resolve such issues and decisions have to be taken on an individual basis. Psychiatrists and physicians have an intuitive repugnance against permitting a treatable respiratory infection or other complication to terminate the life in an aged individual whose emotional responses are relatively well preserved, who seems able to communicate and exhibits a measure of autonomy. Such intuitive reactions have to be heeded, subjective as they are, for they stem from a reverence for the sanctity of life. Once a doctor begins to silence and ignore these signals, he will have become susceptible to other influences. He may begin to allow his judgements about treatment to be shaped by pressures that stem from scant resources, pressures on space and the distress or inconvenience of relatives. All these deserve a place in his total appraisal but it is the plight of his patient which must be accorded the greatest weight and be placed at the focus of his concern. Once he wilts under other influences, he may be prevailed upon at earlier and earlier stages of the illness to wonder whether treatment of Alzheimer's disease, or other dementias, is necessary or desirable. The clinician's desire to heal or relieve illness and suffering and the edge of compassion may be imperceptibly blunted step by step by arguments of expediency.

In the advanced stages of the disease during the last 1–2 years (though in some patients longer), the condition of patients with Alzheimer's disease has many features in common with that presented by patients with PVS. They are bereft of speech or other means of communication. They have neither memory of the past, retention of recent events nor evidence of any intellectual activity. Emotions, whether of pleasure, melancholy, irritation, anger, distress or affection, have all been obliterated. Only a profound and unvarying apathy prevails. A high proportion of patients are bedridden, immobile, doubly incontinent, unable to recognise their relatives or friends or their own reflection in the mirror. They require help with feeding, dressing and they are totally oblivious of their humiliating, totally helpless, condition. This state can be described as vegetative. Owing to weakened gag and swallowing reflexes, part of the food and drink administered passes down the respiratory tract into the lungs. Before the end there may be a period of ravenous appetite accompanied by an incongruous and progressive emaciation.

Neurological signs, including spastic paralysis or a near-Parkinsonian form of rigidity and in a small proportion grand mal fits, make their appearance. Progressive enfeeblement is manifest. When complete and sustained unconsciousness develops at such an advanced stage, in the absence of a definable recent complication, coma soon follows and signals the beginning of the end. The only form of humane and ethical management in the event of an attack of pneumonia or lapse into a coma is expressed in the exhortation 'vex not his ghost'. Attempts to resuscitate such patients restore patients to an existence that is not a life in a real sense. The process of dying should in patients with Alzheimer's disease who have reached this stage be allowed to proceed to the end.

Advance directives or living wills

Living wills enable people to provide advance directives regarding what will happen to them in the event of irreversible disease or provide authority to one person to act on his/her behalf should they become incapable of making decisions regarding the manner in which they will be treated as their lives draw to a close. Living wills began in the course of the 'Right to Die Movement' in the US in the 1960s and were embodied in California's Natural Death Act in 1976. Since that time, 37 states in the USA have enacted 'right to die' legislation[12].

Some advance directives can be judged as authentic, competent and informed after the patient's clinical state has been taken into account and his probable state of mind at the time when the document was drafted has been investigated with relatives or others. In cases of Alzheimer's disease and other dementias, considerations have to be weighed in others deciding on the action to be taken in the event of an acute complication such as the development of a respiratory or gastrointestinal infection, or a descent into coma. The appropriate course may be to allow the patient to die in peace. But pain, restlessness or agitation have to be brought under control with drugs.

However, having regard to the host of problems that have arisen following 'living will' legislation in the USA, it is open to question whether the instructions embodied in such wills should have been accorded compulsory force by law. As the wills are also permitted to specify life prolonging procedures to extend life, physicians are obliged to provide such treatment to the maximum extent possible. The action requested may conflict with the doctor's clinical judgement and ethical standards. The humiliation caused to patients, who may retain some residual awareness of the insensitive procedures entailed in life prolongation, and the distress caused to relatives are also ignored in many living wills. And scant heed is paid to the increasing burden created for the limited resources available. The clinicians' freedom to act in accordance with the condition and the needs of each individual case is undermined.

The freedom and independence with which he can decide and act is also precluded by law. He is unable, in cases of mental deterioration, to consider the circumstances in which the living will was set down and the possible relevance of the course of the illness in the period that has intervened. The directive might, for example, have been formulated soon after the patient's condition was diagnosed as incurable. He may have suffered at the time from a depressive state and been under the influence of nihilistic hopelessness, guilt and suicidal ruminations. In the years or months that followed, his condition might have changed. He may, or may not, have been offered an opportunity to revise his advance directive.

Some individuals, as for example those who suffer from longstanding morbid fears of being buried alive when they are only deeply asleep or suffering from an illness that renders them unresponsive, may prepare a bizarre living will requesting that after death has been diagnosed, they be kept under medical observation for some weeks or months. Permission is accorded for his burial at this stage, that is if no signs of life have been elicited during the stipulated period.

There may be compelling reasons on the grounds of the clinical state of the patient and compassionate concern for the ordeal to which he and his family were being exposed for overriding a directive. Heintz[12] has given a disturbing account of the lengthy and acrimonious legal controversies and struggles that have been generated in every state of the USA by 'right to die' legislation. He points out that poorly drawn wills 'could lead to erosion of patient's rights rather than fulfilment of patients' choice'. He concedes that legislation is required but that 'greater care must be taken to avoid the creation of a Kafkaesque legal nightmare for those we intend to assist'.

Dilemmas in clinical practice common to PVS and Alzheimer's disease and differences between them

For purposes of the comparison to be undertaken in this section, a brief summary of the Judgements pronounced by the Court of Appeal[9] and the House of Lords[11] and the Address by Lord Justice Hoffman should prove helpful. It was made clear and given special emphasis by Lord Justice Hoffman that doctors are morally precluded from taking life with intent. There is no legal sanction for such behaviour even in patients in terminal stages of their illness. A second point lays stress on the qualitative difference between killing and allowing the process of dying to continue without interference. This point deserves some comment from the author. Doctors who offend against this principle will be liable to damage the quality of the personal relationships they can establish with their patients. From being perceived as healers they will also come to be regarded as executioners. For if the physician approaches even demented patients with intent to end life, he is in danger of clouding and confusing his moral judgment. It has been suggested that the fundamental humane sensibilities firmly ingrained in the personality of doctors are modified once they begin to engage in killing[13]. We should have learned from the history of the past century, and the Nazi era in particular, that once they begin to engage in killing, the practice is liable to become habitual and undertaken with progressively weakening stirrings of conscience even in some previously respectable, socially upright persons including doctors.

A third point affirmed that individuals who are completely unconscious and oblivious to persons and the whole world around and capable of neither pain nor pleasure are insensate and have no life to live. They, therefore, need to be protected from further erosion of their dignity and integrity by being allowed to die. Fourthly it was asserted that, in such situations, cessation of medical treatment and artificial feeding should be judged as being neither illegal nor unethical.

The first two principles summarised above are unequivocally relevant for the final vegetative stage of Alzheimer's disease. But in respect of the third, and to some extent the fourth, principle there are significant differences between the two conditions. Alzheimer's disease is the most highly prevalent and far-ranging destroyer of the quality of human life in old age and, if these last two principles were to be uncritically applied to Alzheimer's disease during the greater part of its course, harm could be done on a vast scale.

To quote from Lord Justice Hoffman's statement 'the stark reality is that Anthony Bland is not living a life at all'. This statement was apposite for a patient who had been unconscious owing to PVS for more than 3 years. But it is applicable only to the last chapter of Alzheimer and other forms of dementia which may, of course, drag on for 2–3 painful years and in some cases longer. In the early and middle stages, there may be considerable cognitive impairment, but in her demeanour and emotional interactions she will often be clearly recognisable as the person she was and may need only limited help in dressing and bathing herself.

This point needs to be developed further in the light of one view widely advanced in recent years, that once the personality of a human being has been irreversibly erased he should be judged as suffering from 'brain death'. This is equated by some to death of the person[14] and is implicitly regarded as providing grounds for withholding medication in the case of infection and other illness and avoidance of resuscitation from coma due to some treatable disorder. It was subsequently stated that such steps would be appropriate only for patients in lasting coma. But what criteria are to be employed for determining 'death of personal identity' in the sense used above? The patient with Alzheimer's disease of 3 or 4 years' duration may be incoherent of speech and lacking in understanding and may at times fail to identify her relatives and be intermittently incontinent. During periods of delirium due to acute infection, she may be totally inaccessible. But she usually recovers consciousness if treated. And some are able to smile, express gratitude for a visit with a few words or a surge of pleasure and warmth in the expression of the face which dissolves into a trickle of tears.

Her personality has not irrevocably lost all liveliness, interest and the gift of concern for and involvement with others. From the point of view of integrity of the personality, such patients with Alzheimer's disease are more intact than those with advanced chronic schizophrenia, who exhibit total apathy, inertia, utter incoherent sentences to themselves and emit incongruous giggles or laughter while they sit in isolation from others. No one has suggested for the present that chronic schizophrenics should be allowed to die if they fall physically ill or be submitted to euthanasia. We have no precise or reliable means of establishing end points in personality and self-awareness. There is no one region or specific functional system in the brain where the personality can be located and no investigation with brain imaging or other objective neurobiological assessment that provides a measure of the extent to which personality has been eroded.

It may be that once a firm diagnosis of Alzheimer's disease has been established and the faculty for intelligible communication and understanding have deteriorated, patients with this disease will come to be, and perhaps already are, among those whose lives are involuntarily terminated. If so, medicine and society may have unwittingly wandered onto a slippery slope. It may have moved to a position close to adopting similar practices in patients with Downs syndrome with or without dementia and other forms of mental handicap.

In a proportion of those with Alzheimer's disease, who may appear on routine examination to be totally blank, there may be latent faculties and skills that can be activated to bring to light the survival of distinctive personality features and at times rare and special gifts. This can be illustrated by describing a patient who was aged 80 when first seen. She had been deteriorating for 3 years but remained emotionally responsive and attractive in appearance. Speech was incoherent and memory, orientation and intellect were severely impaired. She was occasionally incontinent of urine. She had been a pianist of distinction since her teens and she continued, despite dementia, to perform the works of classical composers with delicacy and initially with an impeccable technique. The interpretations were all her own, the play of emotion transfigured her facial expression and one had a strong impression that her music played a part in the conservation of her general emotional responsiveness. Four years before she died, she went into coma during an attack of pneumonia. She could have been allowed to die but she was treated and recovered. She continued to play for a further 18 months but with declining skill. She remained, until about a year before death, an affectionate and responsive human being but devoid of cognitive faculties in the last 2 years.

Most patients who suffer from Alzheimer's disease during the last few years are, however, in a kind of vegetative state in which none of their erstwhile personality traits are in evidence. They are bedridden or restricted in mobility, helpless and inaccessible. The only humane course at this stage is to cease medical treatment and to desist from resuscitation from coma or clouded consciousness due to acute infection, cardiac failure or other illness. The crisis in the health services arises to an extent from growing demands that are being made by the rising proportions of elderly who are succumbing to Alzheimer's and other forms of dementia and with disabilities which make large and steeply escalating demands on scant resources. An increasing proportion spend their last years and die in institutions. Some of the apathy, retardation, inattention and even some of the cognitive impairment in the middle phase of the disease arise from the destruction of morale and general stultification generated by the institutional environment. Subsidies to families to enable them to care for their deteriorating relatives to survive for longer periods in their own homes – and to die at home as they used to do until recent decades – might improve the plight of a proportion of those with Alzheimer's disease in their final years. The prevalence of vegetative states among those cared for in a domiciliary setting as compared with those in long term institutions poses a question worthy of investigation.

There is also need for wider emulation of the example set by Cicely Saunders and her followers in the hospice movement in respect of the sense and sensibility with which they care for those in the later stages of progressive mental deterioration, including Alzheimer's disease.

The principles enunciated in the Court of Appeal[8] and the House of Lords[10] provide valuable guidelines for appraisal of the ethical aspects and for the management of the rare disorders with chronic unconsciousness such as PVS. They also shed light on some of the ethical and clinical problems posed by the different kind of vegetative syndrome, manifest during the last few years of Alzheimer's disease. Although some philosophers tend to be sceptical of the distinction between killing and letting die, most doctors must retain the distinction between the two. Their attitude is informed by a moral sensitivity deeply ingrained by ancient traditions and by training and experience, which compels them to 'pause'[15] so often in the course of decision making.

In relation to Alzheimer's disease, the intensity of this moral imperative survives despite all the pressures that impinge on doctors towards its suppression. Doctors are often urged at the present time to 'hasten the process of dying'[16]. To accept this as a general principle would be contrary to ethical sensibility. In the case quoted above, the patient could have been allowed to die of her pneumonia. Letting die could have been defended in the present climate of opinion in a case of well advanced dementia. But her personality was perceived as dignified and inviolable. She continued to evoke affection and transmit it to those close to her. It was judged that to desist from treatment was to give premature sanction to a 'letting die' policy in the management of this patient.

However, in other cases of the same disease, treatment would restore patients to a travesty of life. These cases approximate to the vegetative state which forms the basis of the judgment regarding Anthony Bland in 1992.

For these and other already discussed reasons, the judgments summarised earlier have a more limited application than in the case of PVS for the clinical and ethical problems that have to be resolved during the 3–6 year early and middle stages of the course of Alzheimer's syndrome. For in this disorder, speech, memory, understanding, judgment, independence and personality undergo gradual, rather than suffering instant, obliteration.

There are 600,000 patients affected in the UK and their number is expanding. They constitute a growing medical, social, political and ethical problem of immense dimensions. Neither medicine nor society can remain entirely indifferent to the arguments that flow from scant resources. For this would deny the justice of the claims of children and the young who have to wait for months or years to receive treatment in hospital. But more thought and energy will have to be invested before an equitable and balanced reconciliation of every relevant dimension of the dilemmas that confront medicine and law as also patients, families and society can be achieved.

There is a faint flicker of light in the dark tunnel in which society finds itself. It stems from the rapid advance made by scientific research in the past 10–15 years towards defining the causes of Alzheimer's disease. There is at least some promise that methods of arresting the progress or the disease, and possibly preventing it, may emerge.

References

1 Jochemsen H. Euthanasia in Holland: an ethical critique of the new law. *J Med Ethics* 1994; **20** 212–7
2 Dillmann RJM, Lagemaate J. Euthansia in The Netherlands: the state of the legal debate. *Eur J Health Law* 1994; **1**: 81–7
3 O'Connor DW, Pollitt PA, Hyde JB et al. The prevalence of dementia as measured by the Cambridge Mental Disorders of the Elderly Examination. *Acta Psychiatr Scand<D; 1989; 79*: 190–8
4 Jennet B, Plum F. Persistent vegetative state after brain damage: a syndrome in search of a name. *Lancet* 1972; **i**: 734–7
5 Multi-Society Task Force on PVS. Medical aspects of the persistent vegetative state (first part). *N Engl J Med* 1994; **330**: 1499–508
6 Multi-Society Task Force on PVS. Medical aspects of the persistent vegetative state (second part) *N Engl J Med* 1994; **330**: 1572–9
7 Medical Ethics Committee of the BMA. *Discussion paper on treatment of patients in persistent vegetative state for consultation.* London: BMA, 1992
8 Steinbock B. Recovery from persistent vegetative state? The case of Carrie Coons. *Hastings Cent Rep* 1989; **July/Aug**: 14–5
9 Airedale NHS Trust vs Bland (C A) pp 806–34
10 Airedale NHS Trust vs Bland (Fam D) pp 795–806
11 House of Lords Judgment. Airedale NHS Trust vs Bland (J L (E)) pp 835–99
12 Heintz LL. Legislative hazard: keeping patients living, against their wills. *J Med Ethics* 1988; **14**: 82–6
13 Winch P. The universalisability of moral judgements. In: *Ethics and action.* London: Routledge & Kegan Paul, 1970: p 145
14 Green, Wikler. Brain death and personal identity. *Phil Public Affairs* 1980; **9**: 104–33
15 Gillet G. Euthanasia, letting die and the pause. *J Med Ethics* 1988; **14**: 61–8
16 Miller PJ. Death with dignity and the right to die: sometimes doctors have a duty to hasten death. *J Med Ethics* 1987; **13**: 81–5

Euthanasia in chronic severe disablement

Keith Andrews

Royal Hospital for Neuro-disability, Putney, London, UK

One of the major dilemmas for the clinician caring for people with chronic disabling conditions is how to provide not only a good quality of life but also the best quality of dying. It is my view that the clinician should provide the opportunity for living before giving the opportunity to die. By this I mean that the clinician has the responsibility to ensure that efforts have been made to improve the quality of life by controlling clinical situations and providing psychological and emotional support. Once the decision has been made by patient, family and clinical team that it is inappropriate that life should continue, then the quality of the dying process should be of the highest standard. The present attitude of ending the patient's life by withdrawal of nutrition and fluids is highly unsatisfactory, if not inhumane, and the option of euthanasia would be by far a more satisfactory solution.

In addition, a more satisfactory procedure than application to the High Court for a directive on withdrawal of tube feeding needs to be found. This method is very stressful for family and staff already in distress and is an extremely expensive approach. An independent ethical panel to ensure that the decision to end the patient's life is clinically appropriate, is being carried out purely for the best interests of the patient and is not influenced by the other considerations.

Chronically disabling conditions are common. The OPCS survey of disability in Great Britain (1988)[1] found that 135/1000 of the population had limiting long-standing disability, with the prevalence rate rising from 21/1000 for those 16–19 years of age, through 106/1000 for those 50–54 years, to 779/1000 for those 85 years and over. The Royal College of Physicians' Report (1986)[2], reviewing the literature further, analysed the clinical disorders producing disability and reported that, in a population of 250,000 people, the number who would be severely or very severely disabled would be 860 with arthritis, 115 with respiratory conditions, 340 with stroke, 55 with Parkinsonism and 80 with multiple sclerosis. The Medical Disability Society (1988)[3] reported that there are between 250–375 people in a population of 250,000 with severe or very severe forms of brain damage.

With so many severely disabled people involved, the vulnerability of disabled persons to the disruption of their own self-image, along with the negative concepts to disability by the able-bodied population, makes consideration of ethical issues, including euthanasia, particularly relevant.

Postal address:
Dr Keith Andrews
Director of Medical and
Research Services
Royal Hospital for Neuro-
disability, West Hill
Putney, London
SW15 3SW, UK

British Medical Bulletin 1996;**52** (No. 2):280–288

Terminology

One of the difficulties of discussing the subject of chronic severe disablement is that it covers such a wide range of disorders and attitudes. *Chronic* can include degenerative disorders (such as Huntington's disease or motor neurone disease), conditions which are static for many decades (such as head injury or arthritis), or conditions with a fluctuating pattern (such as multiple sclerosis). Each pattern places a different emphasis on ethical decisions. This is further complicated in that the word 'chronic' is often used nihilistically, meaning 'nothing further can be done'.

Severe is an even more subjective term. The person with paraplegia who is able to tour the world, hold down a job and run a home can be regarded as severely disabled. But severe disability can also be used to describe the patient in late stage multiple sclerosis or Huntington's disease who is totally dependent for all activities and care needs, through to the vegetative patient unaware of the environment yet with the possibility of living for decades.

Disablement is used as a catchall term to cover *impairment, disability* and *handicap*. A severely impaired (e.g. amputee, hemiplegic or blind) person may not be severely *disabled* and certainly not necessarily severely *handicapped*. Since handicap (social functioning) depends on attitude of mind and motivation, rather than on the severity of the impairment or disability, then the quality of life affected by the impairment and disability is more related to mental state, mood, attitude, personality, 'drive' and the environment in which the patient lives. Thus a well motivated person with a constructive personality who is suffering from a 'locked-in syndrome', where there is total paralysis except for the ability to move the eyes, may have a better quality of life than a professional ballerina with chronic arthritis of the knee who is devastated at no longer being able to dance.

This preamble is important in recognising the ethical dilemmas faced by the long-term care physician. The severity of the disability as perceived by the observer may have little correlation with the opinion expressed by the disabled person.

The embarrassment demonstrated by able bodied people in trying to communicate with a severely neurologically disabled person is often expressed as a feeling that the disabled person would be better off dead. The present attitude to 'value for money' and that financial resources should only be used for demonstrable clinical gain, further leaves the disabled person dependent not only on the help but also the good-will of able bodied people. This leads to a lack of self image, depression and expression of dissatisfaction with life.

The ethical problems in chronic disablement are, therefore, not so much to do with the *severity* of physical disablement but with the ability to accept the handicap resulting from the impairment or disability and the influence of society's, usually negative, attitude to disablement. This, however, does give the opportunity, if not the duty, to take every effort to provide facilities to improve the quality of life of even the most severely disabled person. It is ethically essential to give the opportunity to live (in all meanings of the word) before providing the facilities to die.

Clinical ethical issues

Why should a severely disabled person wish to end his or her life? First it is important to emphasise that such expressions of desperation are rare, and usually the reason for the decision is made for very good, though often manageable, reasons.

Severe chronic pain would seem to be the most obvious reason to request euthanasia. Whilst it is not always as easy to control pain as is often stated, pain is often unnecessary because it has not been investigated sufficiently. Analgesia is only one approach to the problem, with much attention required for correct postural control with special seating, good nutrition, overcoming the sensation of general ill health and fatigue, management of depression and splinting of joints. The dilemma arises when there is a need to respond to the patient with intractable pain who requests physician aided termination of life.

Distress at the severity of the disability is another important concern. Ironically, it is often the less severely disabled person who expresses dissatisfaction with life. Very severely disabled people, especially those with brain damage, often do not have the insight into their condition to appreciate their loss. Dissatisfaction with life's lot is, of course, not confined to the disabled population. The request to die may simply be a cry for help.

The third element is the perception of being a burden on other people. There is no doubt that severe disability affects a family as well as the individual. Many families go to enormous lengths to support their severely disabled relative. Others do not have the social, emotional or financial resources to do so. This inevitably places pressure, either overtly or covertly, on disabled persons to recognise that they are a burden. How they respond to this will largely depend on their personality and strength of the family unit.

Whilst these pressures are understandable they are no different from any other clinical situation – they are symptoms for which the cause needs diagnosis and an appropriate treatment started. In chronic disability this is likely to require a combination of social, psychological and recreational, as well as clinical, solutions.

So what are the situations and issues which arise in the clinical management of people with chronic severe disabilities? There are two main situations which arise:

The patient who is severely physically disabled but mentally competent and who does not want to continue to live

This situation is really no different from the able bodied person who does not want to continue living, and probably equally as rare. These patients have the absolute right to make decisions about whether they accept treatment or not. The clinician, however, has the responsibility and opportunity to discuss with them the reasons for their decision, to explain the options open to them and to explain the consequences. In addition, the clinician has the responsibility to ensure that patients are not making the decision to forgo treatment under duress or because they have a treatable condition which is influencing their judgement (e.g. endogenous depression or an acute illness which is making them feel unwell).

Even when the decision has been made to discontinue or withhold treatment, the clinical team are still not in a position to withdraw from the care of the person. They continue to have the responsibility to ensure that the patient is comfortable, does not develop any unnecessary complications, is free from unnecessary distress and remains dignified during the inevitable deterioration into the terminal phase and eventual death. The frustration of helplessness felt by the staff during these phases receives very little attention.

Mentally incompetent patients

Most situations concerning decision making about euthanasia or treatment issues will involve the incompetent patient.

The mentally incompetent patient should have the same rights as the competent person. The decision about whether the patient is incompetent is not always as easy in the clinical situation as it is in the philosopher's chair. This dilemma has been expressed in the Law Commission's *Report on Mental Incapacity*[4]. They give two criteria for the definition of mental incapacity: that the person is 'unable to communicate a decision on the matter because he or she is unconscious or for any other reason'; or that the person is 'unable by reason of mental disability to make a decision on the matter in question'. The difficulty arises when attempts are made to define the ability to 'make a decision'. The Law Commission attempted to clarify this by suggesting two sub-sets – one based on the inability to understand relevant information and the other on the inability to make a 'true choice'. The decision about these issues is far from clear in the practical situation.

Quality of life is a complex concept especially since it is so difficult to measure – what is a poor quality of life for one person may not be for another. Quality of life is subjective and, therefore, no matter what our views are about the level of the quality of someone else's life, the only test is what that person feels. In my experience of working with severely disabled people, I have been surprised by their acceptance of, and ability to cope with, conditions I would have thought to be almost intolerable. Overt depression is not an obvious feature of severely disabled people provided that they have been given the opportunity to function optimally within the limits of their disabilities and in an environment suited to their needs.

One other aspect of this is that I have met several people who have stated, whilst able bodied, that they would not wish to continue living if they developed severe disabilities but who have changed their mind when they found themselves in such a situation. It is almost as though it were easier to understand what it must be like to be dead than have any concept of what it is like to be disabled.

This is particularly relevant since it has been stated that recovering, for instance from the vegetative state, to a severe level of dependency, is 'worse than death'. These statements are made without any research evidence and often by people who have not been involved in the long term management of people with severe disabilities.

Even when the decision has been made that the patient is mentally incapacitated or incompetent, it can be very difficult to know what is in that person's best interest. In any decision about clinical management there has to be a balance between the advantages and disadvantages of the treatment. It goes without saying that the overall benefit must be greater than the disadvantage or harm of the treatment. In complex disabilities this can be difficult, since incomparable benefits and side effects are being evaluated and we are dealing with degrees rather than absolutes.

Discussions about *best interests* have received much attention in cases involving the vegetative state. Here the issue is: 'is it in the best interest of a patient who is unaware of his or her internal or external environment to continue tube feeding?'. The obvious answer may seem to be 'no' but it must be questioned whether the patient has **any** interest rather than a best or worse interest. If this is the case then the decisions are being made for the benefit of others, a dubious decision making process.

Even where the decision has been made to support the patient in life-limiting activities, the options open to the clinician are relatively limited. A do not resuscitate policy is reasonable when discussing cardiopulmonary arrest, but is less helpful when considering other acute medical conditions. If a patient has received good care, then he or she should be in a good nutritional state and, therefore, resistant to infections. Even where infections do occur, withholding antibiotic treatment is just as likely to result in a live, but deteriorated patient, as in causing death. This can hardly be regarded as good clinical management.

The competent patient is likely to be too severely disabled to commit suicide and, therefore, any action by the clinician is assisted suicide. Where the patient is incompetent, then an action, or lack of action, requires a definitive decision by the clinician to assist in the ending of the life of the patient. Whatever semantics are used, withholding or withdrawing treatment will have the same outcome as euthanasia, i.e. the clinician will have taken a decision that the patient should die. This decision is difficult for many clinicians to come to terms with.

The only real option for the clinician, apart from euthanasia, is to withhold food and fluids. There are now several countries where it is accepted, usually after seeking legal declaration in a Court of Law, for feeding tubes to be removed from patients in the vegetative state. This creates several dilemmas for the clinician, even when he feels that the decision is an appropriate one. Whatever the legal view that tube feeding is treatment, there are many carers who regard feeding as care and, therefore, withdrawal of feeding causes them moral, ethical and practical problems.

Having decided that it is appropriate that the patient should die, then there is a reluctance to be seen to take an active part in the ending of the life. We cling to the concept that food is a treatment. Since the 'treatment' is futile, we can, therefore, stop the treatment and the patient will die due to the brain damage. To assuage our own emotional needs, we then decide to starve and dehydrate the patient over a period of 10–14 days until he or she dies of 'natural' causes. The argument, that since the patient cannot feel discomfort from this treatment, then the slow mode of death is acceptable, denies the respect we have for a dying person. Even a dead person is treated with respect and we would not carry out acts on a dead body simply because they would not be felt. Society is, therefore, in a dilemma – it is of the opinion that the patient should die, but it does not want a quick death because that would be seen as euthanasia.

The decision to withdraw or withhold feeding in the vegetative patient is difficult, but the situation becomes more difficult when dealing with the patient who is aware but profoundly disabled. This can be seen, for instance, in deciding whether to place a gastrostomy tube in a patient with Huntington's disease, where the condition is deteriorating and the patient is cognitively impaired, and dysphagic. In this situation certain questions have to be asked:

1. If the tube is not placed, what will the consequences be to the patient?
    a. Will the patient be able to get sufficient food or fluids if additional care is taken and more time is available to feed the patient?
    b. Is the patient choking at frequent intervals.
    c. Is the patient losing weight rapidly?
    d. Is the patient developing pressure sores?
    e. Will the patient become dehydrated?

2. What is the progression of the disorder the patient is suffering from?
    a. Is the patient suffering from a rapidly deteriorating condition?
    b. Will tube feeding merely delay the natural terminal stages of the illness?

3. What effect will tube feeding have on the quality of life of the patient?
    a. Will it enable the patient to have less distressing bouts of choking?
    b. Will it enable the patient to feel better?
    c. Will it enable pressure sores to heal in a patient who is not in the terminal stages of illness?
    d. Will tube feeding merely prolong an already unhappy, unsatisfactory or distressing life?
    e. Will tube feeding merely prolong 'existence' in a patient who is unaware of his or her surroundings?
    f. Will tube feeding give the opportunity to see if optimal conditions will allow the patient to make some recovery?

There is growing support for the concept of advance directives in assisting with the decision making on behalf of incompetent patients. There is, indeed, much advantage as far as the clinician is concerned in accepting advance directives at face value. The difficult decision can be taken out of the hands of the clinical team, since they are simply obeying the wishes of the patient. It helps to overcome difficulties in the case of the incompetent patient, where there are differing views amongst members of the family or where the family have taken a position which is at variance to that of the clinical team. It also makes it easier for the decision to be made when there are differing opinions as to appropriate action amongst the members of the clinical team.

The strength of the advance directive is its ability to provide help to the clinician in the end-of-life treatment decisions. But, in chronic disability, we are often not dealing with terminal events and, therefore, the concerns become quality of life, or dying, issues – a much less objective field of clinical evaluation. The purpose of an advance directive is to give the incompetent patient the same rights of decision making as the competent patient, as discussed above. However, advance directives are often made without the opportunities for informed consent required for the competent patient. Concerns include:

Informed consent   On what basis did the patient make the decision that he or she would not want to be treated? The decision not to accept treatment should be based on clear understanding of the situation. It is therefore essential that the patient really understood the disorder. This can be complicated in rarer conditions, such as vegetative state for instance, where the clinician giving the advice has very little experience, if any, of the condition and is, therefore, not knowledgeable enough to give informed guidance.

Opportunity to change mind   In a patient who is mentally alert and who makes a decision not to receive treatment, there is always the opportunity for the clinician to sit down with the patient and discuss the reasons for the decision in the light of the particular clinical features of that patient. The clinician also has the opportunity of discussing with the patient why he or she does not want treatment. Is it fear of pain, of loss of dignity, concern for others, etc.? In these circumstances, the clinician is, therefore, in a better position to ensure that the patient has clearly thought out the decision. This possibility is removed when faced with an advance directive and an incompetent patient.

Potential for scientific development   Competent patients have the advantage of making their decision based on up-to-date knowledge. Advance directives may be made many years prior to the time for their implementation, during which period new treatment or changes in quality of life opportunities may have occurred.

Clarity of the advance directive   Advance directives are not always clear about the intention of the patient. For instance, I have seen a recent advance directive which stated that, if the person developed severe brain damage, she would not want to continue living. There was no statement as to whether this decision was to be made on the first day or after a period of several days/weeks/months to give the opportunity of recovery. The definition of *severe* brain damage gives great opportunities for widely differing opinions, even amongst clinicians experienced in the management of brain damage.

One major difficulty for the chronic care physician is 'who should make the decision that it is not in the patient's best interest to receive treatment?'. Whilst it is usually recommended that the family be involved in the discussion about the management of the incompetent patient, they do not have the legal authority for deciding what is in the best *clinical* interest of the patient. Since *treatment* requires a clinical decision, the family, whilst expressing opinions, do not have the final say in the treatment. When the issue is care, as opposed to *treatment* (though the distinction is not always obvious), then the position of the clinician is less clear.

Whilst relatives may be in the best position to advise on the views that the patient would have expressed, there is always the concern that they may be transferring (consciously or otherwise) their own opinion of the situation. Inevitably, disabilities affect a family rather than just the individual and, therefore, there are dilemmas in deciding what emphasis to put on the relatives' views. This is even more complicated when, not uncommonly, there are differing views within the family.

References

1 Martin J, Meltzer H, Eliot D. *The prevalence of disability among adults*. Report 1. London: HMSO, 1988
2 Royal College of Physicians. Physical disability in 1986 and beyond. *J R Coll Physicians Lond* 1986; **20**
3 Medical Disability Society. *The management of traumatic brain injury*. London: Medical Disability Society, 1988
4 Law Commission. *Mental Incapacity Law Communication No 231*. London: HMSO, 1995: pp 36–8

Euthanasia: the intensive care unit

John F Searle

Department of Anaesthesia, Royal Devon and Exeter Hospital, Exeter, UK

The purpose of intensive care is to provide monitoring and organ support for patients with critical illness from which recovery is possible. Despite increasing technological and pharmacological sophistication, mortality in intensive care units remains high, with significant disability in those who survive.

Methods of predicting outcome from intensive care have been developed. These enable patients to be placed in risk groups, but do not accurately predict the outcome of individual patients. That prediction is a clinical judgement based on the underlying disease, the number of body systems failing and the length of time for which intensive care support has been necessary.

Once a decision has been made to withhold or withdraw intensive care, the principles of good palliative medicine should be employed during what will then be the inevitable terminal phase of the illness.

What is intensive care?

A modern intensive care unit (ICU) contains a large amount of sophisticated equipment. It is staffed by highly trained doctors and nurses who are supported by an extensive network of technicians and other health workers. The first major step in the development of ICUs was taken by Lassen in 1951 when he used positive pressure ventilation to treat respiratory failure caused by poliomyelitis[1]. Since then, several attempts have been made to define intensive care. It is essentially a service for patients with potentially recoverable diseases who can benefit from more detailed observation and treatment than is generally available in standard wards and departments[2]. It involves intensive patient monitoring both clinically and technologically. Such monitoring either detects the early failure of body systems, thereby enabling intervention to prevent further deterioration, or when organ failure has already occurred monitors the effectiveness of treatment[3]. Central to intensive care is the support of body systems by machines and drugs. Inevitably, therefore, patients in ICUs are highly dependent and constitute a huge work load for those who look after them. ICUs contain the most critically ill patients in a hospital but the question is, 'does recovery actually take place?' What is the outcome of adult intensive care?

Postal address:
Dr J F Searle
8 Thornton Hill
Exeter EX4 4NS, UK

The outcome of intensive care

Early studies of the outcome of intensive care looked at deaths within units. However, it was obvious that these figures did not give an accurate picture of outcome but that hospital mortality, mortality after discharge and the quality of life of survivors needed to be considered. Initial attempts were made to do this in the UK and North America by reviewing the outcome of patients treated with mechanical ventilation[4-6]. 50% of patients died before leaving hospital and a further 10–19% survived for less than 1 year. Only one-in-five of all patients had returned to their previously normal life 12 months after leaving hospital.

More recent studies in the UK of all patients admitted to ICUs continue to show a high mortality with 52% of patients being alive 2 years after leaving intensive care[7]. Many of those who survive have a reduced quality of life. In American and European studies, mortality varied from 18–69%[8]. This wide range reflects the nature of intensive care case mix in different units. Nevertheless, the early and late mortality of patients requiring intensive care is high. What is the cost of such a death rate?

The cost of intensive care

It has been known for many years that the cost of intensive care is very high and that the cost per case for nonsurvivors is much greater than for survivors[9]. The cost per patient day is 4–5 times that of an acute general ward[10]. In one London hospital, the total cost of intensive care over 40 months was £10 million: 36.8% of this was spent on 15.5% of patients who died[11].

Is such a distribution of resources just? Does expenditure on nonsurvivors divert resources away from other areas of health care? If intensive care beds are occupied by patients who are not likely to survive are other patients who would benefit from intensive care denied it?

Reports in the media in 1995 about intensive care services in the UK gave no reassurance about the answers to these questions.

However, the cost of futile intensive care is not only financial but also human. Where survival is very unlikely the process of dying is prolonged. False hopes are raised for the relatives as well as drawing out their anxiety and distress. Staff may become demoralised as they realise that, despite their efforts over many days and sometimes weeks, death is inevitable.

The cost of inappropriate intensive care has been summarised by Jennett[12]. It may be: unnecessary because the same end could be achieved by simpler means; unsuccessful because the condition is beyond influence;

unsafe because the risks of complications outweigh the probable benefits; unkind because the quality of life afterwards is unacceptable; unwise because resources are diverted from more useful activities.

There is, therefore, a responsibility on intensive care specialists to direct their skills and resources to those who are likely to recover. Indeed, it is the potential for recovery which should be the criterion both for admission to an ICU and for continued intensive care treatment[2]. In trying to exercise this responsibility several questions arise. Is it possible to distinguish between those patients who will recover and those who will not? How accurate is the science of prognosis in intensive care? Is it possible to know when intensive care treatment is increasing the chance of survival or simply prolonging dying? Can we be as confident as the old woman pauper in Oliver Twist who declared that she knew 'when death's a coming'?

These questions have exercised the minds of doctors and others for more than two decades. 'The issue of life versus death is placed in sharper focus than ever before because our ability to keep people alive for weeks or more with critical illness has improved greatly with advances in technology. Those of us who are placed in positions of responsibility and leadership for the care of the critically ill are forced to make decisions which may involve discontinuing support[14].'

Predicting outcome in intensive care

Predicting the outcome of disease has long been part of medical practice. The outcome of malignant disease is formulated on the basis of clinical trials and series of cases, as the percentage of patients with a given stage of the disease surviving after a specified number of years. Some of the earliest attempts to predict outcome in critical illness were made in head injuries[14], and in non-traumatic coma[15]. These were particularly important in helping clinicians decide whether or not to continue with intensive care treatment in patients with severe brain damage as they made it possible to quantify the risk of death and severe disability.

However, while critical illness may be precipitated by major trauma or a single underlying disease, usually several body systems are affected. This is more pronounced where there is also chronic disease, such as ischaemic heart disease and irreversible obstructive pulmonary disease. Predicting outcome in these circumstances requires the construction of a profile of the patient's disordered physiology. Several attempts have been made to do this but the one that has featured most prominently in recent years is the acute physiology and chronic health evaluation or APACHE, developed by Knaus and his colleagues at the George Washington

University Medical Center to study ICU outcome and utilization and evaluate new therapies[16,17].

In the commonly used APACHE II system, a score of 0 to 4 is assigned to each of 11 objectively measured physiological variables. Points are also assigned to the Glasgow Coma Score, the patient's age and precisely defined chronic health status. The system is independent of therapy, valid over a wide range of diagnoses and is based on data available in most hospitals. There is a clear relationship between the APACHE II score and the risk of death. In its original validation in 5815 patients in 13 ICUs[17], there was a predictable increase in death rate for each 5 point increase in the score. Thus, with a score of 5–9 there was a death rate of 3.9% rising to 84% for scores greater than 35. The underlying disease was a major factor in determining the risk of death. In congestive cardiac failure, for example, there was a risk of death of 13% with a score of 10–19. This risk doubled for the same score in septic shock.

A similar pattern was found in a multicentre study in the UK of over 9000 ICU admissions, although there were differences in the case mix between units[18]. The APACHE system stratifies critically ill patients into risk groups. It does not allow the risk of death for individual patients to be predicted. As one commentator has pointed out, 'a predicted risk of death of 50% identifies a critically ill population but it also tells us that for any patient within that mortality band the outcome could not be more uncertain'[19].

Several attempts have been made to formulate more precise methods of predicting outcome. Knaus carefully defined organ-system failure for the cardiovascular, respiratory, renal, haematological and neurological systems[20]. In a study of 5677 ICU patients in 13 hospitals, 2140 patients (38%) had one or more organ-system failure on admission and a further 579 (16%) developed organ-system failure after admission. Outcome depended on the number of organ-systems failing and the length of time for which they had failed. 80% of patients with more than three systems failing during the first 24 hours of admission died (20% of course, surviving). But if a three system failure continued for more than four days, all the patients died.

Another approach has been to perform an analysis of the daily trend in the APACHE score[21]. These trends have been combined in computerised programmes with the organ-system failure score and adjusted for specific diagnostic categories and used to refine prediction further[22]. However, even these sophisticated systems have a false positive rate. In a study from Guy's Hospital, of 137 patients predicted to die, 6 survived[11]. In another unit, 119 patients were predicted to die but, of these, 24 were discharged home[23]. Furthermore, scoring systems are not very sensitive. In the Guy's study, for example, although 137 out of 3702 patients were predicted to die, 560 actually died.

Thus, while scoring systems are a useful tool for audit within and between ICUs, a recent European Consensus Conference rightly concluded that they are an inadequate basis for making treatment decisions about individual patients already in ICU or for conducting a preadmission triage[24]. However, scoring systems do give a pointer towards the direction in which a patient is moving. They provide clinicians with more knowledge about groups of patients than they can ever hope to acquire in their own practice. They also identify the factors which must be considered in making decisions about individual patients.

Age is an important factor. Older patients do less well than younger ones. The underlying pathology is crucial as prognosis is different for different conditions. The number of body systems failing, and the degree of technological and pharmacological support they require, also have a profound effect on outcome. Most important of all is time. Each day a careful assessment should be made and the question asked, 'is this patient's condition improving or deteriorating?' A progressive deterioration over several days in the face of intensive care support is an indication that such support is prolonging dying rather than saving life.

The decision to withdraw intensive care treatment in the expectation that death will follow is an informed judgement. In our present state of knowledge, it cannot be more than that.

The management of terminal illness in ICU

It is helpful to discuss the decision to withhold or withdraw intensive care treatment with all those involved in the patient's management. The general practitioner often contributes important information about the patient's previous quality of life as well as much wisdom about what is appropriate in patients they have known for many years. In this way an informed consensus is arrived at.

Because the onset of critical illness is usually rapid, the patient's wishes are mostly not known. Clouding of consciousness by the underlying disease or by drugs used necessarily in intensive care makes it difficult to establish what those wishes are. Advance directives do tell clinicians what those wishes were, but they still leave them with the task of identifying when intensive care is futile and, therefore, of when to comply with the directive. Hence discussion with those close to the patient plays an essential part in the decision making. While for incompetent patients the doctor alone may lawfully decide what is in the patients best interests[25], relatives need both to understand and accept when continuing intensive care is indeed futile.

The principles of terminal care in an ICU are the same as those in palliative medicine. Their adaptation to terminal critical illness was described a decade ago[26,27]. As technological and pharmacological support are withdrawn, adequate doses of opioids and other drugs should be used to prevent pain, breathlessness, the accumulation of secretions and other distressing symptoms. Particular problems occur when patients are dependent on mechanical ventilation with high concentrations of inspired oxygen and/or high doses of inotropic drugs. Rapid withdrawal of these results in almost immediate death which, from the point of view of the relatives, may seem indecently sudden. The reduction of the concentration of inspired oxygen and/or the dose of inotropic drugs over a few hours gives the relatives time to say 'goodbye' and in being supported by staff, begin their bereavement.

Conclusion

Is to withhold or withdraw intensive care and change the direction of care to the relief of symptoms, euthanasia? Certainly death in such circumstances is quiet and dignified (it is a common misconception that death in an ICU is unseemly and undignified). But the fact is that when life-sustaining treatment is stopped death does follow. The alternative is to continue to employ all the resources of intensive care and to treat each new complication as it arises. Such a process may sometimes go on for weeks. The question is which course of action best reconciles a doctor's duty to benefit patients but not to harm them and to use resources effectively for the many but not thereby disadvantaging the few?

Acknowledgements

I am grateful to Dr Julia Munn and Dr James Rogers for their help in the preparation of this paper.

References

1 Lassen HCA. A preliminary report on the 1952 epidemic of poliomyelitis in Copenhagen, with special reference to the treatment of acute respiratory insufficiency. *Lancet* 1953; **298**: 37–41
2 King's Fund Centre for Health Services Development. Intensive care in the United Kingdom: report from the King's Fund Panel. *Anaesthesia* 1989; **44**: 428–31
3 Association of Anaesthetists of Great Britain and Ireland. *Intensive care services – provision for the future.* 1988
4 Searle JF. The outcome of mechanical ventilation: report of a five year study. *Ann R Coll Surg Engl* 1985; **67**: 187–9

5   Nunn JF, Milledge JS. Singaraya J. Survival of patients ventilated in an intensive therapy unit. *BMJ* 1979; **279**: 1525–7
6   Editorial. Intensive-care audit. *Lancet* 1985; **330**: 1428–9
7   Ridley S, Jackson R, Findlay J, Wallace P. Long term survival after intensive care. *BMJ* 1990; **301**: 1127–30
8   Dragsted L, Qvist J. Epidemiology of intensive care. *Int J Technol Assess Health Care* 1992; **8**: 395–407
9   Cullen DJ, Ferrara C, Briggs BA, Walizer PF, Gilbert J. Survival, hospitalisation charges and follow up results in critically ill patients. *N Engl J Med* 1976; **294**: 982–7
10 Ridley S, Biggain M, Stone P. Cost of intensive therapy. *Anaesthesia* 1991; **46**: 523–30
11 Atkinson S, Bihari D, Smithies M, Daly K, Mason R, McColl I. Identification of futility in intensive care. *Lancet* 1994; **344**: 1203–6
12 Jennett B. Inappropriate use of intensive care. *BMJ* 1984; **289**: 1709–11
13 Skillman JJ. Ethical dilemmas in the care of the critically ill. *Lancet* 1974; **ii**: 634–7
14 Jennett B, Teasdale G, Braakman R, Minderhoud J, Heiden J, Kurze T. Prognosis of patients with severe head injury. *Neurosurgery* 1979; **4**: 283–9
15 Levy DE, Bates D, Caronna JJ et al. Prognosis in nontraumatic coma. *Ann Intern Med* 1981; **94**: 293–301
16 Knaus WA, Zimmerman JE, Wagner DP, Draper EA, Lawrence DE. APACHE – Acute physiology and chronic health evaluation: a physiologically based classification system. *Crit Care Med* 1981; **9**: 591–7
17 Knaus WA, Draper EA, Wagner DP, Zimmerman JE. APACHE II: a severity of disease classification system. *Crit Care Med* 1985; **13**: 818–29
18 Rowan KM, Kerr JH, Major E. McPherson K, Short A, Vessey MP. Intensive Care Society's APACHE II study in Britain and Ireland. 1: variations in case mix of adult admissions to general intensive care units and impact on outcome. *BMJ* 1993; **307**: 972–7
19 Bion J. Outcomes in intensive care. *BMJ* 1993; **307**: 953–4
20 Knaus WA, Draper EA, Wagner DP, Zimmerman JE. Prognosis in acute organ-system failure. *Ann Surg* 1985; **202**: 685–93
21 Chang RWS, Jacobs S, Lee B, Pace N. Predicting deaths among intensive care unit patients. *Crit Care Med* 1988; **16**: 34–42
22 Chang RWS, Jacobs S, Lee B. Predicting outcome among intensive care unit patients using computerised trend analysis of daily Apache II scores corrected for organ system failure. *Intensive Care Med* 1988; **14**: 558–66
23 Hope AT, Plenderleith JL. The Riyadh Intensive Care Program mortality prediction algorithm assessed in 617 intensive care patients in Glasgow. *Anaesthesia* 1995; **50**: 103–7
24 Chang RWS, Le Gall JR. Predicting outcome in intensive care unit patients. Second European Consensus Conference in Intensive Care Medicine. *Intensive Care Med* 1994; **20**: 390–7
25 F vs West Berkshire Health Authority [1989] 2 All ER HC
26 Grenvik A. 'Terminal weaning'; discontinuance of life-support therapy in the terminally ill patient. *Crit Care Med* 1983; **11**: 364–5
27 Searle JF. Terminal weaning. *Crit Care Med* 1984; **12**:1010

Palliative medicine: a new specialty changes an old debate

James Gilbert

Postgraduate Medical School, University of Exeter, Exeter, UK

The specialty of palliative care, of which palliative medicine is part, has developed from hospice care for the dying and aims to meet the various needs of those suffering from advanced incurable progressive disease. Specialist palliative care is not expensive and can be made available to all those who need it, at home, in hospital or in a hospice. Arguments in favour of permitting euthanasia for those dying as a result of a chronic disease are usually based on compassion, respect for autonomy or perceived hypocrisy in existing medical practice. Each of these arguments is examined and found wanting.

A little imagination and time to reflect is enough for most people to be able to think of circumstances sufficiently awful to justify ending the life of a fellow human being on grounds of compassion. The certainty of having no means of relieving extreme suffering – most obviously in wartime, but perhaps not exclusively so – will on occasion make euthanasia the only possible moral response. In peacetime, in the developed world, such occasions are very rare. I shall examine whether such occasions are so rare, or we can make them so rare, as to deliver us of the need to allow lawful intentional killing on grounds of compassion. The question of justifying euthanasia on grounds of respect for autonomy will be considered separately.

What is palliative care?

Palliative care is needed by all those suffering from advanced progressive incurable disease. It is provided by relatives or other informal carers and by health care professionals both generalist and specialist. Palliative medicine refers to that contribution to the practice and study of palliative care which is made by doctors. The definition which was adopted in 1987, when palliative medicine was recognised in Britain as a medical specialty, states that 'palliative medicine is the study and management of patients with active, progressive, far-advanced disease for whom the prognosis is limited and the focus of care is the quality of life'. The

*Postal address:
Dr James Gilbert
Exeter and District
Hospice, Dryden Road
Exeter EX2 5JJ, UK*

Oxford Textbook of Palliative Medicine provides a comprehensive overview of current practice[1]. The World Health Organization defines palliative care as follows[2]:

> The active total care of patients whose disease is not responsive to curative treatment. Control of pain, of other symptoms, and of psychological, social and spiritual problems is paramount. The goal of palliative care is the achievement of the best possible quality of life for patients and their families.

Palliative care:

- affirms life and regards dying as a normal process
- neither hastens nor postpones death
- offers a support system to help patients live as actively as possible until death
- offers a support system to help those close to the patient cope both during the patient's illness and in their own bereavement.

The study and specialist practice of palliative care stems from the modern hospice of which the first is generally acknowledged to be Saint Christopher's in Sydenham, London, UK. The thirty or so years since the opening of Saint Christopher's Hospice has seen a considerable expansion of specialist palliative care services both geographically and in terms of how and where care is offered. The successful provision of specialist palliative care requires a team including nurses, social workers, clergy and other therapists and the ability and determination to work together as a team. The success of specialist palliative care is also dependent on working effectively with generalist colleagues in the primary health care team and with colleagues in hospital-based specialties.

Can effective palliative care be made available to all those who need it?

The usual objection to the assertion that effective palliative care is an alternative to permitting euthanasia on grounds of compassion is that hospices are too small to cope[3], rather than that symptoms in advanced disease cannot adequately be relieved. We shall return to the question of adequate relief later in this chapter but first; are hospices too small to cope? A description of the clinical activity of the charity 'Hospiscare', the provider of specialist palliative care for a population of about 300,000 in the south-west of England, will demonstrate how services **can** be made sufficiently available[4]. The requirement is for homecare, daycare, in-patient care, out-patient consultation and hospital support.

Homecare

To serve the stated population, much of which is widely spread, a total of 19 clinical nurse specialists in palliative care work in teams of two or three with and alongside primary health carers in each locality. Appropriate care is provided in the home, in residential or nursing homes and in community hospitals ensuring that expertise in the control of distressing symptoms is available to all who need it. An equally important function of this home care service is to allow the opportunity for sensitive honest communication about the implications of the advancing disease. The widely varying degrees of truth appropriate for different individuals and families, up to and including outright denial, are respected. Careful, unhurried listening is required to achieve this. Social and financial problems are addressed by the Hospiscare social workers who also co-ordinate and supervise continuing support for families and other carers into bereavement. Practical help with transport needs and in the home is given by over a hundred volunteers organised by a part-time paid volunteer co-ordinator.

The Exeter and District Hospice

The hospice building is located centrally in the health district within the grounds of, but separate from, the district general hospital. The hospice offers both in-patient and day care and acts as the focus of integrated specialist palliative care by providing comprehensive clinical, educational and managerial support to the district-wide homecare service. Clinical nurse specialists attend weekly educational meetings and have access at any time to the hospice doctors for advice and support. The medical director is also available for out-patient consultations and is jointly employed by the adjacent general hospital trust as consultant in palliative medicine. Specialist palliative care for those dying from advanced progressive incurable disease in the general hospital is the shared responsibility of the consultant in palliative medicine and the relevant hospital-based clinical nurse specialist who is also employed by the charity Hospiscare.

The population actually reached

Of the 1000 or so people who die from cancer in the district annually, Hospiscare contributes to care in about 700 cases. There is no discrimination against those with diagnoses other than cancer and about

30 people with other terminal illnesses are also cared for annually. Having contact with such a large proportion of the population in potential need of admission enables the hospice in-patient unit to be used for those genuinely in the greatest difficulty. Approximately 300 people are admitted each year and the majority are discharged home when symptoms are adequately controlled. The average length of stay is 1 week. The preponderance of cancer diagnoses probably reflects both the kinds of problems encountered for which palliative care is an appropriate response and historical factors in the development of hospices.

The cost

The overall annual cost (for a population of 300,000) of the comprehensive integrated district-wide service described is less than £6 per head. The fact that more than half of this total is donated voluntarily demonstrates the importance attached to this part of health care by the general public.

In considering the extent to which good palliative care can be a valid alternative to permitting euthanasia, it has been necessary to examine local experience with a particular service in some detail. We should turn now to some wider issues.

Limitations to palliative care

It has been shown above that comprehensive specialist palliative care can be made available at modest cost to all those who need it, irrespective of diagnosis. The hospice experience of the last three decades is that when high quality care of this type is provided to those with advanced progressive incurable disease, the demand for euthanasia on grounds of compassion disappears. A description of how this is achieved follows later but, before proceeding, two important limitations need to be examined.

Religious exclusivity

Feeling excluded from palliative care (particularly that provided in hospices) for religious reasons is a problem more for those in potential than actual need. Even the most overtly religious hospices are at pains to make clear that those of any faith, and those of none, are welcomed. It must, however, be acknowledged that the widespread perception that hospices are religious foundations is based on the truth of their specifically Christian origins. The importance of ensuring that services are genuinely sympathetic and 'user friendly' to those of other faiths has been acknowledged and addressed recently by the National Council for Hospices and Specialist Palliative Care Services[5]. Many modern hospices have no religious orientation but are clearly aware of the need to address the spiritual, if not religious, concerns of those who know that they are approaching the ends of their lives. This religious neutrality of hospice care has sound theological justification; it is not merely a necessary accommodation to life in a secular society[6]. A concern which is occasionally expressed, but which I believe is groundless, is that in some hospices physical symptoms may be incompletely relieved because of a belief in the value of sharing in Christ's passion.

Medium-term institutional care

If religious exclusivity is an unnecessary and increasingly infrequent limitation to effective and available palliative care, the provision of satisfactory medium-term institutional care may be becoming a more frequent problem. Specialist palliative care as described is not concerned with the provision of medium-term (by which I mean many weeks) continuous nursing care for those who may be highly dependent but have continuing but stable needs. As the population of developed countries ages such needs are growing. It is fundamentally important to the question of permitting euthanasia to separate the issue of resource allocation into at least two parts. Satisfactory palliative care comes at modest cost much of which is born by voluntary donation. However, no matter how completely physical, psychological and spiritual needs can be met by means of palliative care, we could as a society condemn people to such poor nursing and social care as to create a persistent rational demand for euthanasia. As a policy this would be anathema to those proponents of euthanasia who are primarily concerned with human dignity, but the possibility exists that by default requesting euthanasia could become the lesser of the available evils. The proper way to answer people who express the view that their advancing illness has resulted in their feeling a burden to their carers or to society is not to deny the reality but to make clear that, as in infant-hood or temporary illness, the burden is one that collectively we wish to shoulder.

Why is the illegality of euthanasia not a problem?

The organisation for which I work contributes to the care of 700 people per year and each one is dying from an incurable progressive disease. It is very widely known that no-one in the district with palliative care needs, be they intractable pain or other physical symptoms, psychological distress or spiritual suffering, will be refused help. Almost always hospice admission can be arranged on the day of request and never with more than a few days' delay. Despite this close involvement with the very patients for whom euthanasia is advocated we do not encounter **any** persistent rational demand.

I am aware that this statement will surprise many people and that it may be disbelieved. Certainly the subject is not avoided in palliative care[7]. The wish for 'it all to be over' is sometimes expressed and, more rarely, 'if I was a dog you would put me down'. When sensitively explored, however, such expressions of distress have never amounted in our experience to a clear repeated request to have a lethal injection administered. A recent illustrative example is of a man who talked repeatedly about ending his own life and about how wrong it was, in his view, that euthanasia was not legally available to him. His desire to express in this way his distress at physical deterioration was accompanied by a determination to continue with medication to maintain normal calcium levels, without which he would probably have died sooner. Such contradictory messages from patients with advanced disease are not unusual. The importance of separating persistent rational requests for euthanasia from strong expressions of distress is hard to overstate. Severe seasickness, for example, may transiently make one wish one were dead. If such a time-limited and benign source of physical distress can engender such feelings, the utmost care must be taken in interpreting statements which could be seen as requests for euthanasia. There are a number of possible explanations for the observed lack of persistent rational requests for euthanasia in palliative medical practice.

If euthanasia is illegal there is no point in asking for it

Although superficially attractive as a possible explanation, there are good reasons to doubt it. Most importantly knowing that an act is illegal is not likely readily to dissuade a desperate person from asking. Certainly **repeated** refusal may in the end dissuade, but the reality in advanced incurable progressive disease is that requests are not repeated if true needs are properly addressed. It is often heard in public debate that doctors **do** secretly administer lethal injections. Of course the real frequency of such desperate action cannot be gauged, but the hospice experience is that it is never necessary. The fundamental and clear distinction between treating symptoms fully with whatever doses of therapeutic medication are required and the deliberate administration of a lethal drug is examined below.

Pain, other symptoms and other suffering can always be completely controlled

Unfortunately this is not true. The possibility is sometimes held out of sufficient opportunity, resource and perseverance in palliative care research eventually allowing distress-free human dying. Since pain clearly has important emotional and psychological as well as sensory components, and since dying is often simply tragic it seems inevitable that suffering and dying will for ever be linked. The notion that euthanasia must not be permitted because palliative care research would be thereby retarded amounts to requiring the dying to act as an experimental substrate. Not only Kant[8] would find this idea objectionable.

Sufficient help can always be given to enable people to live with their distress

The willingness to administer successively larger doses of medication in response to worsening symptoms (dose titration) is a consistent feature of palliative care. The fact that there are times when the medication required may itself cause a shortening of life has led to doctors being charged with hypocrisy. The crude allegation is that poisoning people with pain relieving or sedating drugs is on occasion held to be good medicine, but using a drug such as potassium chloride, which is rapidly and reliably toxic to the heart, is immoral. The truth is that poisoning people by whatever means is immoral. The distinction is to be found not in the choice of drug but in the certainty in the effect of potassium chloride and inherent uncertainty when titrating therapeutic drugs against symptoms. Of course to be morally significant this uncertainty must be genuine. The argument that only some members of a firing squad are given live ammunition may be psychologically significant but is unconvincing morally. No, there is good evidence that this uncertainty when using dose titration is quite genuine. Examples may help: (a) a doctor called to testify in the case of Dr Bodkin Adams asserted that a particular dose (of opiates) must certainly kill, only to be told that the patient had previously been given that dose and had survived[9]; (b) accidental administration of diamorphine far in excess of the intended dose has been associated with no ill effects[10]; or (c) pain acts as the physiological antagonist of the respiratory depressant effects of opioid analgesics[11].

Despite this demonstrable uncertainty there are many well intentioned doctors, some very experienced in other areas of clinical practice, who relate instances of having given medication to desperately ill patients who died soon after (see, for example, Henderson[12]).

The impression given is of a compassionate doctor who knows the result of the action taken and disregards the personal legal risk. Those with the most extensive experience of looking after the dying know that one cannot know the outcome of such action. The truth is that these decisions are more mundane than they are portrayed to be but unfortunately the image of doctors as courageous and omniscient is seductive to public and profession alike. In these circumstances it is certainly possible that the known side effects of certain treatments (e.g. strong opioids) might result in *earlier* death than if such treatment were reduced or withheld, but it is equally possible that sufficient (and no more) treatment of pain and other symptoms might bring about a physical state in which the patients' other resources allow them to live *longer*.

The orthodox view is that, because sufficient treatment to control symptoms should be given, the shortening of life is seen as an acceptable by-product. But, in fact, there is no evidence that good palliative care shortens life and I believe, though I concede I cannot prove, that sufficient treatment given for serious symptoms associated with advanced disease is as likely to *prolong* life. It may therefore be that invoking double effect is unnecessary, even counter productive.

In palliative care, the uncritical application of medical technology is avoided

Being kept alive by means which are seen as intrusive and undignified when the quality of the life which is thereby sustained is too poor to be valued is a fear which underlies some support for euthanasia. It is to be hoped that a clear code of practice[13] giving guidance about the drafting and implementation of advance statements about medical treatment (living wills) will reduce these fears. The palliative care approach attaches great importance to the avoidance of intrusive medical interventions, unless improved quality of life is clearly likely to result. It has recently been argued that hospice practitioners are on occasions wrong to avoid medical interventions such as artificial hydration[14], but there are well reasoned refutations of this position[15,16].

Why is autonomy in fact so rarely exercised?

Suicide is very uncommon in those suffering from advanced incurable progressive disease[17]. National figures are inadequate to allow comparison between rates of suicide among people with cancer and others and there is likely to be some under-recording among those with very advanced illness. However, one might reasonably expect a clear excess of deaths by suicide among a group who have both the means (easy access to strong drugs) and a genuine desire for an early death. The proportion of cancer sufferers who are truly physically unable to commit suicide is tiny and the question of being psychologically unable to do so is addressed below. Other possible explanations include:

Because the enormous majority of references made to euthanasia by the dying are never intended to be taken at face-value

The fact that euthanasia is known to be illegal allows discussion of the issue to be used safely to express strong feelings. Effective response to such expression may take several different forms. Efforts to control physical symptoms may need to be redoubled, perhaps enlisting help from colleagues. Often it is the minimising of dependence and the maximising of dignity which is being sought. Most frequently, however, it is reassurance of their continuing worth as a person that is the real reason for patients suggesting that they would be better off dead. How often in our daily lives do we feel the need to say that we have to leave in order to find out whether our hosts want us to go?

Because even those few who seriously intend to take their own lives keep on putting it off

The hospice experience generally is that quality of life which seems completely inadequate to the healthy onlooker is in fact almost always valued highly and clung to tenaciously[18].

Because suicide is usually a solitary act, and used to be illegal and is seen by some as immoral and by others as cowardly

For the above reasons many people have insuperable psychological difficulty in committing suicide. To help them over such difficulty it would be necessary to agree that their life is no longer worth living and endorse the acceptability of the proposed action. There is a subtle but crucial impasse here. One can never know whether agreeing that a person's life is no longer worthwhile and giving the endorsement which is sought may be decisive in bringing about an unnecessary and tragic act. Perhaps it is for this reason that to assist in suicide is a criminal offence. I do not regard suicide as necessarily immoral or cowardly, but sadly I believe there is good reason for it to be a solitary act.

From whom do most requests for euthanasia actually come?

People imagining their own future suffering

If the extent to which good palliative care is effective and available is not known (or not believed), future uncontrolled suffering may be an understandably potent fear. Those in whom progressive illness has been diagnosed will be especially vulnerable to such fear. It is, therefore, literally vital that information about prognosis is balanced and based on real experience rather than speculation. Perhaps because historically doctors have been guilty of giving false reassurance, a determination 'not to make light of the situation' may raise unrealistic fear. In a recent Dutch television film showing an act of euthanasia, the doctor concerned predicted, to a man with motor neurone disease, end-stage complications which were never in fact encountered in the largest series of deaths from this disease in the world's medical literature[19].

Relatives and friends who find the dying of their loved one terrible to witness

It might be argued that many people are so insulated from the realities of death and dying that the abilities of previous generations to cope have atrophied. Widespread euthanasia may produce an increasing need to sanitise dying as opposed to a healthier acceptance of dying as part of living.

Relatives and friends wishing in retrospect that things could have been different

Proponents of euthanasia frequently give descriptions of the last days of a loved one. Such descriptions, as recalled, can be harrowing and often raise important questions about the type and standard of the professional care which was apparently offered. When considered in retrospect, it may seem clear that death would have been welcome some hours or days before it came. As an argument for euthanasia the logical difficulty lies in identifying in advance how close death is. The popular view that doctors can predict prognosis with any accuracy, **even in very advanced disease,** is a myth[20]. All distress in those close to death needs full treatment and those about to be bereaved often also need professional support, but it is not logical to request the removal of the last biscuit in the packet on the grounds that it often gets broken.

Is there a useful distinction to be made between rational autonomy and blind autonomy?

Over the last few decades in the developed world, fewer and fewer deaths have occurred at home with the result that most people have become unfamiliar with death and dying. At the same time, advances in medical technology have at times brought about unintentional prolongation of dying rather than saving of life. Much of the current desire to permit euthanasia can be attributed to very rational fears either of uncontrollable suffering at the end of life or of the unwanted and undignified prolongation of very poor quality of life. Rational autonomy should be respected and fears such as these can genuinely be allayed without permitting euthanasia. Those for whom unfettered autonomy is a goal in itself may be much the minority but will not be dissuaded from seeking legal change to permit euthanasia no matter how much dignity and comfort can be brought to the dying. Indeed, those whose desire for autonomy is blind in this way presumably seek euthanasia on demand.

Conclusion

The Dutch experience is that, despite detailed legal guidelines, euthanasia is administered to those who neither request it[21] nor have terminal illness[22]. The extent to which this should alert the rest of the world to the dangers of permissive legislation is for others to discuss. In this paper, I have sought to demonstrate that if there is any necessity to permit euthanasia, it is not in order to improve the way that we care for those with advanced incurable progressive disease.

Acknowledgements

I have benefited from discussing ethical issues with many friends and colleagues. I would particularly like to thank John Ellershaw, Thurstan Brewin, Derek Doyle, Andrew Goodman, Richard Gilbert, Anna Morris, and my teachers in the Philosophy Department of the University of Swansea.

References

1   Doyle D, Hanks GWC, Macdonald N. *Oxford textbook of palliative medicine*. Oxford: Oxford University Press 1993: p 3
2   World Health Organization. *Cancer pain relief and palliative care*. Technical Report Series 804. Geneva: WHO, 1990
3   Editorial. The final autonomy. *Lancet* 1995; **346**: 259
4   Gilbert J, Hancock JR, Anning PA. *Hospiscare management plan and service profile*. 1993. (Unpublished, but available from the authors at the Exeter and District Hospice)
5   National Council for Hospice and Specialist Palliative Care Services. *Opening doors: improving access to hospital and specialist palliative series, No. 7*. London: 1995
6   Dunstan GR, Marshall J, Seller MJ. Hospice care: a Christian perspective. *Palliative Med* 1991; 5&D:: 187
7   Seale C, Addington-Hall J. Euthanasia the role of good care. *Soc Sci Med* 1995; **40**: 581–7
8   Kant I. *Groundwork of the metaphysic of morals*. Paton HJ. (trans). New York: Harper and Row, 1964
9   *Report of the Select Committee on Medical Ethics*. Session 1993–94, House of Lords Paper 21-I
10 O'Neill WM. Safety of diamorphine in overdosage. *Palliative Med* 1989; **3**: 307–9
11 Hanks GW, Twycross RG. Pain, the physiological antagonist of opioid analgesics. *Lancet* 1984; i: 1477–8
12 Henderson S. Euthanasia: the dilemma of the decade. *The Independent* 7 December 1994
13 *Advance statements about medical treatment*. Report of the British Medical Association. London: BMJ Publishing Group, 1995
14 Craig GM. On withholding nutrition and hydration in the terminally ill: has palliative medicine gone too far? *J Med Ethics* 1994; **20**: 139–43
15 Ashby M, Stoffell B. Artificial hydration and alimentation at the end of life: a reply to Craig. *J Med Ethics* 1995; **21**: 135–40
16 Dunlop RJ, Ellershaw JE, Baines MJ, Sykes N, Saunders CM. On withholding nutrition and hydration in the terminally ill: has palliative medicine gone too far? A reply. *J Med Ethics* 1995; **21**: 141–3
17 *Submission from the Ethics Group of the Association for Palliative Medicine of Great Britain and Ireland to the House of Lords Select Committee on Medical Ethics*. Association for Palliative Medicine Occasional Paper, May 1993, Appendix 2, p 23
18 Twycross RG. *Pain relief in advanced cancer*. Edinburgh: Churchill Livingstone, 1994: p 554–5
19 O'Brien T, Kelly M, Saunders C. Motor neurone disease: a hospice perspective. *BMJ* 1992; **304**: 471–3
20 Heyse-Moore L, Johnson-Bell VE. Can doctors accurately predict the life expectancy of patients with terminal cancer? *Palliative Med* 1987; **1**: 165–6
21 Pijnenborg L, van der Maas P, van Delden JJM, Lowman CWN. Life-terminating acts without explicit request of patient. *Lancet* 1993; **341**: 1196–9
22 Spanjer M. Mental suffering as justification for euthanasia in The Netherlands. *Lancet* 1994; **343**: 1630

Euthanasia: the institutional response

Ann Sommerville

British Medical Association, London, UK

For health institutions, euthanasia represents an increasingly complex but increasingly inescapable debate, in which the expectations of health professionals have moved away from the declaratory answer in search of greater sophistication and clarity. The House of Lords' Committee on Medical Ethics drew attention to the unavoidable complexity of future medical decisions at the end of life, the inexorably changing doctor-patient relationship and the demographic shift resulting in greater numbers surviving longer to face chronic, degenerative conditions. The committee proved a watershed in many respects, not least in the moral debate it triggered in the public and among health professionals. Arguably it aired questions which still have not been conclusively answered. Its questioning mirrored the trend observable among the institutions' membership for rigour and detail to justify the positions adopted. It represents one facet of the pressure on health institutions, whose previous mode of dealing with the euthanasia debate was by declaration and some would say by pontification. Their reticence to probe deeper was undoubtedly based partly on the conviction that detailed debate about euthanasia was an anathema within professional groups committed to the traditional life-preserving goal of medicine. Also influential has been the assumption that it would be otiose for professional bodies to issue guidance on matters unambiguously covered by law. Arguably, both of these views should have been challenged if not dispelled by the effort involved in contributing evidence to the House of Lords' Committee. That exercise exposed the need for guidance and the ambiguities at law but it remains to be seen how the debate will be taken forward, or not, by health institutions.

N.B. Views given are those of the author not the BMA

Awareness of evolving practices in The Netherlands and a string of English legal cases, from Bodkin Adams (1957) to Leonard Arthur (1981) and Nigel Cox (1992), have kept euthanasia at the forefront of British medico-legal debate. There have been calls for Parliament or a Royal Commission[1] to review the law and attempts made to introduce Bills[2] to amend it. Euthanasia is guaranteed to provide polemic at medical ethics' conferences and students' debates. Surveys reporting trends in the opinions of the public at large or health professionals in particular constitute a recurring feature in professional journals. Nevertheless there is confusion. Patients' legitimate right to decline life-sustaining treatment is still sometimes conflated with euthanasia, including by some members of Parliament[3]. Most discussion about euthanasia, however, defines it as

*Postal address:
A Sommerville, British Medical Association, BMA House, Tavistock Square, London WC1H 9JP, UK*

a voluntarily and persistently requested active medical intervention whose principal intention is to end life. This is the meaning attached to euthanasia here, although it should also be noted that the potential for progression from voluntary to involuntary and non-voluntary euthanasia forms a persistent undercurrent of much recent debate.

Analysis of the 'institutional response' to the debate depends partly on the inclusiveness or exclusiveness of the term 'institutional'. A variety of official and quasi-official organisations are potentially eligible. My remit is to focus primarily on the regulatory bodies which govern medicine and nursing and the associations which represent health professionals nationally and internationally. To lend context to the substance of their views, however, brief reference is also made to the published comments of some institutions with less singular responsibilities, such as the House of Lords, the Church of England and the Department of Health. In addition, much of the detailed commentary on euthanasia has come from groups which fall outside the common perception of the category of 'institutions' but whose publications deserve mention not least because their views are, in some cases, as likely to be influential as those of the professional bodies.

Despite the apparently widespread tide of interest in euthanasia and abundance of material from non-official sources, the response of medical and nursing institutions has seemed, until recently, conspicuous by its absence. Indeed, the statutory body for nurses (the UKCC) has said that 'the need for debate and serious consideration of these issues has been stifled and obstructed by concealment and a lack of candour'[4]. An exception to the general institutional taciturnity was a report by a British Medical Association[5] (BMA) working party in the late 1980s, which after examining some of the main arguments, supported retention of the criminal penalty for euthanasia. The report attracted criticism at the time for its paternalistic tone and alleged equivocal handling of complex points but it represented an attempt to initiate institutional debate. That apart, the lacuna evident until recently in the publications of British institutions has reflected a similar omission in those of international bodies. The 1994 draft Bioethics Convention of the Council of Europe[6], for example, while giving considerable attention to most other aspects of medical duties and patient rights – (to the extent of commenting on how discarded human hair and fingernails could be sold without affronting human dignity) – contains no explicit reference to the intentional termination of human life.

Nor is evidence of the relatively thin institutional comment on euthanasia restricted to Britain or Europe. The bulletin of the French Medical Association (*Ordre des Medecins*)[7] published a survey in March 1994, indicating how few articles were available in the medical literature internationally before 1974. It noted an increase in interest resulting in 24 polls of medical practice and opinion in eight countries between 1980 and 1993. None of the quoted articles or surveys conducted in those 13 years, however, appears to emanate from a professional body. They were primarily conducted by medical journals, academic centres or branches of the Voluntary Euthanasia Society.

Even when institutional comments on euthanasia have been available, these have traditionally taken the form of position statements and declarations rather than dialectic or moral discourse. A brief, two-sentence statement categorising euthanasia as unethical was published in 1987 by the World Medical Association[8] (WMA), but provided no supporting reasons for that stance. Similarly, in 1992, the WMA condemned physician-assisted suicide as unethical. In the same year, the Royal College of Nursing published a position statement, declaring 'the practice of euthanasia is contrary to the public interest and to medical and nursing ethical principles as well as to natural and civil rights'[9]. This may be seen as typifying the traditional declaratory, rather than explanatory, approach of health bodies.

The fact that in Britain there is now a recent collection of institutional views on euthanasia is due primarily to that most venerable and archetypal British institution, the House of Lords. Members of the Lords, sitting as ultimate appellate court in the 1993 Bland case, were obliged to confront a number of philosophical as well as legal concepts, including the distinction between killing and letting die. The case turned on whether withdrawal of nutrition from an incapacitated individual, inevitably resulting in his death, constituted a lawful act. The Lords decided that withdrawal of artificial feeding would be an omission, a failure to act, a 'letting die', but would not constitute the offence of homicide. Lord Browne-Wilkinson, however, summed up an apparent anomaly germane to the case:

> How can it be lawful to allow a patient to die slowly, although painlessly over a period a weeks from lack of food but unlawful to produce his immediate death by a lethal injection?[10]

Although the Lords agreed that this was indeed the current legal position, the perplexity inherent in Browne-Wilkinson's question hung in the air to haunt the subsequently established House of Lords' Select Committee on Medical Ethics.

In the spring of 1993, this committee called for individual and organisational views on care and treatment at the end of life, eliciting among the responses a profusion of comments from bodies representing health professionals. Among those who responded were the statutory body for nurses, the United Kingdom Central Council for Nursing, Midwifery and Health Visiting (UKCC), the Conference of Medical Royal Colleges, the Department of Health, the multi-disciplinary

National Council for Hospice and Specialist Palliative Care and three professional associations: the British Medical Association (BMA), Royal College of Nursing (RCN) and Association for Palliative Medicine. They were invited to submit commentary on the ethical, legal and clinical implications of patients' refusal of life-prolonging treatment and the possible circumstances in which actions designed to shorten a patient's life might be justified.

Questions circulated in advance by the Lords' committee centred on the principal moral and legal issues which had exercised philosophers and lawyers as well as their lordships in the Bland case. Most of these issues, however, were not matters health bodies had previously explored in print. They included consideration of the sometimes conflicting moral principles of personal autonomy and the sanctity of life, the distinction between withholding medical treatment and a deliberate medical intervention to end life and the different considerations arising for mentally competent and incompetent individuals. The written and oral evidence produced in response and published by the House of Lords[11] in 1994 provides the most comprehensive summary of the current views of the main UK health bodies on euthanasia and related issues.

Nevertheless, given the prominence accorded to the intricacies of the arguments by philosophers, lawyers, patients and journalists, the previous paucity of published advice on euthanasia specifically addressed to those people most frequently asked to administer it, seems surprising. When invited to consider specific questions regarding their policies on euthanasia, health bodies exposed some gaps in what might otherwise have appeared a seamless web of healthcare provision at the end of life. Both of the bodies representing nurses, the UKCC and RCN, took the opportunity of expressing objections to the way in which medical opinion sometimes ignored or subverted the contribution of nurses[12] in end-of-life decisions. Good communication between health professionals themselves and as a component of supportive patient care was seen by all health groups as an important ideal, not always achieved in practice. Most health bodies were opposed to the legalisation of euthanasia. The main endorsement for the idea of new legislation came from the UKCC, which, while not specifically supporting euthanasia, called for sensitive legislation to allow 'professional practitioners the opportunity to identify and serve the best interests of their patients'. In its evidence to the Lords, the UKCC did not specify the type of legislation required or how 'best interests' might be defined but indicated an open attitude on these points. This was also the organisation most critical of the lack of clear guidelines to deal with the complex legal and ethical maze in which health professionals found themselves.

All health institutions accepted competent patients' rights to decline life-prolonging treatment as a facet of respect for autonomy. Most also saw a valid moral distinction between a medical decision to withhold futile treatment ('letting die'), professional actions which shorten life as an incidental consequence of ensuring patient comfort (the principle of 'double effect') and the intentional terminating of a patient's life. Only the latter was regarded as 'euthanasia'. The other options were generally classified as acceptable facets of good professional practice. The UKCC, however, considered the act and omissions distinction rather discredited and expressed reservations, which many of its members were said to share, about the validity of the principle of 'double effect'. The distinction between 'killing or letting die', which the medical bodies generally supported was considered to be frankly hypocritical by the UKCC which was undoubtedly the most outspoken body in challenging the otherwise broadly accepted views of professional bodies.

Some support for the UKCC view was forthcoming from the English and Welsh Anglican and Catholic Bishops who issued a joint statement[13]. While recognising that medical treatment could be morally withdrawn or withheld if treatment was disproportionate in terms of its painfulness, intrusiveness, risk or costliness in relation to the expected therapeutic benefit, the Bishops nevertheless envisaged cases where 'withholding treatment might be morally equivalent to murder'. They opposed the legalisation of euthanasia but rejected the notion of conflict between the concepts of sanctity of life and personal autonomy since, they said, there can be no obligation to keep seriously ill patients alive at all costs. The Board of Responsibility of the Church of Scotland also published a booklet on euthanasia in 1995[14] which saw no theological difficulty in allowing patients to die naturally and depicted good terminal care as the best solution to requests for euthanasia, which it unreservedly opposed. The Churches, like most of the health professionals, also considered that personal autonomy could not constitute an absolute right but should be considered in relation to other moral values. In their emphasis on the sanctity of life as a God-given gift and the view 'that the Christian recognises no right to dispose of his own life'[15], the Churches diverged from the health professional organisations.

The secular nature of the responses from health professional organisations is worthy of note. It may be contrasted with the approach taken by the BMA's report of 1988 which devoted a chapter to religious and humanist perspectives while acknowledging that 'the religious conviction which underlay the concept of sanctity of life is no longer a universally accepted basis for medical practice'[16]. In response to the Lords' committee in 1993, however, several health bodies in answering the question on the concept of sanctity of life drew specific attention to non-religious values attached to the phrase and emphasised the pluralistic and multi-cultural background within which terminal care is currently provided.

Interestingly, the Lords' committee's own response to the moral questions raised echoed a prominent line of argument adopted by many of the health bodies in that it was essentially pragmatic. The committee did not accept the possibility of setting secure limits on the practice of voluntary euthanasia if the law were to be changed and considered it impossible to frame adequate safeguards against non-voluntary euthanasia or other abuses creeping in. While acknowledging 'that there are individual cases in which euthanasia may be seen by some to be appropriate', the committee insisted that 'individual cases cannot reasonably establish the foundation of a policy which would have such serious and widespread repercussions'[17].

This did little to alleviate the profound dilemmas experienced by some health professionals since it simply appeared to distil a mass of wide-ranging opinions into what was arguably a self-evident conclusion: i.e. that euthanasia may appear appropriate in some cases but is illegal. Guidance on how to handle the cases where euthanasia might apparently be 'appropriate' has not been forthcoming. Furthermore, from the evidence provided to the Lords by the palliative care bodies, one is left with the abiding sense that health professionals, working intimately with the dying, feel frustrated that the wrong questions are sometimes being asked by theoreticians with little experience of the realities and complexities which occur in terminal care.

The key institutions for health professionals are the regulatory bodies: the General Medical Council (GMC) for doctors and the United Kingdom Central Council for Nursing Midwifery and Health Visiting (UKCC) for nurses. The GMC was placed under a statutory obligation by the *Medical Act, 1978* to give ethical advice and set standards and the role of both bodies includes the training and disciplining of their members. The only specific comments on euthanasia from the GMC were published in November 1992, when it was required to examine the actions of Dr Nigel Cox who had been found guilty of the attempted murder of a patient by administration of a lethal substance. In its statement, the GMC did not attempt to probe the moral arguments but simply reminded doctors of their duty to obey the law. The Conference of Medical Royal Colleges and Faculties[18] have also steered clear of the issue. Hippocratic values and the clear legal prohibition of euthanasia have been seen as obviating the need for guidance or prolonged institutional debate. It is interesting to note, however, that although the traditional wording of the Hippocratic oath clearly prohibits the administration of 'deadly medicine', when the WMA came to restate the oath in modern terms in the Declaration of Geneva, it referred only to a general respect for human life and 'laws of humanity'. The Geneva Declaration contains no specific mention of euthanasia.

Nevertheless, it appears that doctors are not only asked to limit or withhold treatment but also to practice euthanasia. Rising figures have been documented in surveys and medical willingness to discuss them appears also be increasing[19]. It has been claimed[20], for example, that as many as one doctor in two in some parts of western Europe is likely to face a request for euthanasia at some point. Excluding The Netherlands, where different legal provisions apply, Belgian GPs may be among the most frequently approached European professional group[21]. In Britain too, if the perennial and complex 'end of life' queries to the BMA are representative of the uncertainty of health professionals, there is a need for professional guidance which goes beyond declarations or statements of illegality. Most particularly, doctors appear to echo some of the UKCC statements in their concern about how boundaries are to be drawn between acceptable measures which accelerate dying; non-treatment or non-resuscitation which may have the same effect; and intentional termination of life. Additional misgivings often arise about philosophical arguments differentiating treatment of autonomous individuals and non-autonomous beings, such as handicapped neonates or people who are permanently unconscious. Health professionals frequently appear to want guidelines which incorporate elements of intuitive correctness as well as logical consistency and intellectual rigour. Whether health institutions are able to satisfy these demands in the future remains to be seen.

The BMA responded to the changing needs in 1993 by publishing discursive commentary and advice on 'care for the dying' and 'cessation of treatment, non-resuscitation, aiding suicide and euthanasia'[22]. In this publication, it maintained its anti-permissive stance on euthanasia, this policy having been established and repeatedly confirmed in open debate at its membership conferences. The justifications for the policy were discussed, including the premise later endorsed by the Lords' committee that the risks of tolerating euthanasia in even a few individual cases might outweigh the benefits by having a negative impact on the whole fabric of society and potentially introducing additional pressures on the elderly and sick to avoid being a public or family burden.

As noted previously, many of the detailed contributions to the euthanasia debate have been provided by groups other than professional institutions. The Linacre Centre, for example, established in the late 1970s to promote study of health care ethics within the Catholic moral tradition, published a study[23] of euthanasia in 1982 which discussed five areas of care where questions of medical termination of life arise. It concluded that involuntary euthanasia was systematically practised on viable handicapped neonates (principally by omission of life-saving procedures) and active euthanasia was practised but seldom prosecuted in cases of terminally ill patients. The report found no evidence of either euthanasia or medical attitudes favouring it in relation to handicapped adults, the elderly and people in intensive care units, but noted that both undertreatment and overtreatment were equally common in geriatric wards. It argued against euthanasia on the grounds of the enduring value of human life but recognised some circumstances in which the curtailment of burdensome treatment would be morally justifiable.

Following the BMA's 1988 report, the Institute of Medical Ethics established a working party to consider the ethics of prolonging life and assisting death. It provided a counter-point to the BMA's views in its report[24] of 1990, suggesting that 'assisted death' should be acceptable in certain clinical situations. It concluded that 'a patient's sustained wish to die is a sufficient reason for a doctor to allow him to do so' and that 'a doctor acting in good conscience is ethically justified in assisting death if the need to relieve intense and unceasing pain or distress caused by an incurable illness greatly outweighs the benefit to the patient of further prolonging his life'. The report's thoughtful evaluation of the primary ethical principles and its wide dissemination in the *Lancet* undoubtedly contributed to the trend towards increasing sophistication in the institutional debate.

Academic and inter-disciplinary publications have also doubtless influenced British opinion and practice. A notable example is the Appleton Consensus[25] of the late 1980s, which established widely accepted 'guidelines for decisions to forgo life-prolonging medical treatment'. The consensus document, produced by an international, multi-disciplinary group, set standards for many aspects of decision making but left open the desirability or otherwise of 'statutory legalisation of the intentional termination of life by doctors'. While rejecting active euthanasia of permanently incapacitated people, it stated that requests from competent but incurably ill patients for medical assistance in dying 'may be morally justifiable and should be given serious consideration'.

Finally, the contributions of patient representative groups cannot be overlooked. The Voluntary Euthanasia Societies in particular have published prolifically their predominantly rights-based and utilitarian arguments. Their surveys and widely disseminated newsletters appear to attract a growing membership and exercise an influence on public opinion.

References

1 See for example, Smith R. Euthanasia: time for a royal commission *BMJ* 1992; 305: 728–9. In the Lords' hearing of the Bland case, both Lord Browne-Wilkinson and Lord Mustill identified a need for Parliamentary review
2 See for example the *Voluntary Euthanasia Bill* introduced by P Khabra, MP on 10 June 1993
3 See for example, early day motion by David Alton MP on Withdrawal of Treatment, 10 February 1994 and Parliamentary debate on Euthanasia, 19 April 1995, *Hansard* p 150-170

4 Written evidence from the United Kingdom Central Council for Nursing, Midwifery and Health Visitors to the House of Lords Select Committee on Medical Ethics, vol II, p 142, para 31

5 *BMA report on Euthanasia, 1988.* The report was updated by the BMA in its 1993 publication *Medical Ethics Today*

6 *Draft Convention for the protection of human rights and dignity of the human being with regard to the application of biology and medicine: Bioethics Convention and explanatory report.* Council of Europe, July 1994

7 Kenis Y. L'euthanasie active et les medecins: practiques et opinions. *Bulletin trimestriel du Conseil National, Ordre des Medecins*, vol III, no 63, March 1994, Paris

8 *World Medical Association Declaration on Euthanasia*, adopted by the 39th WMA meeting in Madrid, October 1987, published in the WMA Handbook of Declarations, October 1994

9 Royal College of Nursing Council paper, March 1992

10 Lord Browne-Wilkinson, Airedale NHS Trust v Bland, [1993] All ER 884

11 Select Committee on Medical Ethics, vol II written evidence. London: HMSO, 1994

12 Evidence to the House of Lords Select Committee on Medical Ethics, vol II, pp 75, 155

13 Joint press statement and submission from the Church of England House of Bishops and the Roman Catholic Bishops' Conference of England and England, 8 July 1993

14 *Euthanasia–a Christian perspective.* Edinburgh: Board of Responsibility of the Church of Scotland, 1995

15 *Euthanasia–a Christian perspective.* Edinburgh: Board of Responsibility of the Church of Scotland, 1995: p 4

16 *BMA report on euthanasia.* p 41, para 148

17 *Report of the Select Committee on Medical Ethics* vol 1. House of Lords, p.48, para 237

18 Brief oral comments were, however, made by Sir Douglas Black to the House of Lords on behalf of the Conference or Royal Colleges and their Faculties, 4 May 1993, published in vol II of the House of Lords' report

19 For example, Ward BJ, Tate PA. Attitudes among NHS doctors to requests for euthanasia. *BMJ* 1994; **308**: 1332–4; *Survey of Colorado physicians.* Hastings Centre, 1989; 19(1); Kuhse H, Singer P. Doctors' practices and attitudes regarding voluntary euthanasia. *Med J Aust* 1988; **148**: 623; Mapi. Sondage aupres de 455 generalistes. *Le Quotidien du Medecin* 1990; **4553**

20 Kenis Y. L'euthanasie active et les medecins: practiques et opinions. *Bulletin trimestriel du Conseil National, Ordre des Medecins, vol III* no 63, March 1994, Paris

21 A 1984 survey conducted by *Le Journal du Medecin* indicated 69% of Belgian GPs reported receiving requests for euthanasia although it must be noted that the sample population was small (100 doctors) and self-selecting. Vankeerberghen JP. Resultats du referendum du *Journal du Medecin. J Med* 1984; **234**: 2

22 These topics form chapters 5 and 6 of the BMA's publication, *Medical Ethics Today*, 1993

23 *Euthanasia and clinical practice: trends, principles and alternatives.* London: The Linacre Centre, 1982

24 Report of the Institute of Medical Ethics working party on the ethics of prolonging life and assisting death. *Lancet* 1990; **336**: 610–3

25 The Appleton Consensus was drawn up by a multi-national group meeting in Appleton, Wisconsin in the late 1980s. Their consensus document was first published in the journals of three Scandinavian Medical Associations in 1989 and in Britain by the *Journal of Medical Ethics* in 1989 and 1992, (supplement to vol 18)

Euthanasia and the law

Margaret Brazier

Faculty of Law, University of Manchester, Manchester, UK

This paper examines why the law concerns itself with euthanasia. The nature of the right to life and its protection in law is explored. Such a right demands legal intervention to prohibit, or at least control, involuntary and non-voluntary euthanasia. Voluntary euthanasia is not a violation of the individual's right to life as such, so on what grounds can law limit autonomy by prohibiting such conduct? It is suggested that, while concepts of sanctity of life still play a part in the legal debate, fears of abuse in any scheme for voluntary euthanasia largely explain the reluctance of many jurisdictions to follow the example of The Netherlands. Finally, the paper asks whether reform and regulation of voluntary euthanasia are as attractive options as they are sometimes portrayed.

Euthanasia in its original, literal meaning, a gentle and easy death, is what we all hope or pray for. The law plays no role in euthanasia if good fortune or good medicine allows such a death. Today, however, euthanasia all too often attracts a second meaning[1], an act or omission designed to hasten death and thus relieve the suffering of a dying or incurably sick patient. The law immediately rears its ugly head in its most awful guise. Has the perpetrator of such an act or omission committed the crime of murder? Other chapters of this issue explore the substantive laws of the UK, The Netherlands, Canada and the USA. Cartwright analyses the validity of any distinction made between killing and letting die. Ann Somerville examines the response to the euthanasia debate of organisations such as the British Medical Association. This chapter seeks only to investigate why law should concern itself with euthanasia. Dying is our inevitable fate. Family, friends and health professionals may be expected to help us meet that fate. Who wants a lawyer at the death bed?

A right to life

Postal address:
Professor M Brazier,
Faculty of Law, University
of Manchester, Oxford
Road, Manchester
M13 9PL, UK

'Everyone's right to life shall be protected by the law'[2]. The right to life is the fundamental human right. Absent that right, all other rights to liberty, privacy, family life and so on are meaningless. No qualification attaches to that right. Society may not demand that a human being achieve a set level of intellect or ability to assert that right to life. The multiply disabled individual unable to care for herself in any sense, the terminally ill centenarian are as much entitled to that right as the healthy and distinguished editors of this Bulletin. The law's legitimate interests in protecting that right thus justifies legal intervention to prohibit (or at least control) involuntary and non-voluntary euthanasia.

Involuntary euthanasia, in the sense of conduct designed to end the life of someone who desires to go on living, is hardly worthy of debate. A lethal injection to kill a tetraplegic perceived as a burden to her relatives and the health care service is morally indistinguishable from common murder. It matters not whether the homicidal act is carried out by spouse or doctor. Yet are the barriers against involuntary euthanasia as watertight as appears to be the case at first sight?

In most jurisdictions today, the unborn human entity can be killed. The handicapped foetus in England may be destroyed at any time up to live birth[3]. The right to life only crystallises at birth. The Downs syndrome infant who survives the perils of her mother's womb cannot be actively destroyed any more than can her tetraplegic aunt.

Assume for the moment though, an ability on the part of both to express a wish to live. May they be let die against their will? Certainly withholding most routine treatments would contravene the law as much as would active killing of the patient. But what of expensive, complex therapies? Recently, in England, the father of a young girl suffering from leukaemia was refused further treatment for her by the local health authority. He believed cost to be a factor in refusing treatment to his child, that her right to life was just too expensive to protect. The Court of Appeal declined to intervene[4].

Non-voluntary euthanasia, defined as conduct designed to end the life of someone who has never expressed any wish either to die or survive, and who cannot currently communicate any desires of his own, is equally a legitimate concern of the law. Neither extreme youth nor age, disease nor profound disability qualify the right to life, yet nor do they qualify the right to compassion. The patient's condition may be such that prolonging life simply extends suffering. There are nearly always some means available to extend life, to prolong the process of dying. The law is unlikely to, and would be wrong to, demand that all available means be employed to do so. When an infant, known only as C, was born with an exceptionally severe degree of hydrocephalus, was blind and deaf and became unable to feed naturally, the English Court of Appeal held there was no mandatory obligation to resort to nasogastric or intravenous feeding[5]. The medical evidence was that the child would not survive more than a few more weeks whatever was done for her. The professionals' duty was to alleviate her suffering by all means short of actively ending her life.

More difficult than C's case is the scenario where a patient is not imminently dying but is irreversibly afflicted by a condition from which he cannot recover. J was another infant born profoundly handicapped. He suffered acute brain damage at birth. He was likely to develop paralysis, blindness and deafness. His condition caused episodes of cyanosis and collapse. The baby was successfully resuscitated on at least two occasions. Given intensive care and treatment he could live into his teens. The Court of Appeal was asked if J suffered a further collapse, must he be resuscitated[6]? The court said no. The best interests of the child must be evaluated. The court must attempt to assess the 'assumed' view of J and take full account of the instinct to survive. There would nonetheless be cases, and J's was such a case, where 'it is not in the interests of the child to subject it to treatment which will cause increased suffering and produce no commensurate benefit'[7].

The tragedy of Tony Bland is well-known. Crush injuries at the Hillsborough football stadium left the youth in a persistent vegetative state. He could breathe independently but all his other bodily functions and needs had to be met artificially. He received food and water via a nasogastric tube. Ultimately the English courts were asked whether it would be lawful to cease feeding the young man. For so long as artificial means maintained the necessary nutrition and hydration he would go on 'living' perhaps for several more years. The House of Lords found that it would be lawful to cease feeding Tony Bland and 'allow him to die'[8]. Once again the court maintained an absolute prohibition on involving any 'external agency of death'.

The rights and wrongs of the judgments in *Bland* will be debated later by McCall Smith. Two points need to be made here about *Bland* and all other instances of non-voluntary euthanasia.

1. Clearly the law rightly concerns itself in such cases. The individual cannot assert or protect his own right to life, cannot balance the benefits of existence against non-existence for himself. The law plays a proper role in protecting him. How far formal external mechanisms to fulfil that role are needed may be disputed. The law must calculate how far society may reasonably entrust the protection of the patient to his family or his doctors.
2. The fundamental question posed by the operation of the law in such cases, however, is **why** maintain a prohibition on active killing. Once it is conceded a patient no longer benefits from life, why not end that life swiftly and mercifully?

A right to die?

Did Tony Bland, and the infants C and J have a right to die? No such right is articulated in the US Constitution, or the United Nations

Declaration on Human Rights, or the European Convention on Human Rights. Before returning to such cases of non-voluntary euthanasia, the so-called 'easy' case of voluntary euthanasia should be explored. If the willing patient may not be killed at his express request, clearly no other category of patient can be said to have a right to be killed. But, if a competent patient freely and fully understanding the consequences of her choice wishes her life to end, what business is it of the law's to interfere with her autonomous choice?

As later chapters will illustrate, in practical terms a right to die may well depend on the accident of exactly what kind of condition precipitates a patient's wish to die. A competent patient generally enjoys an absolute right to refuse further treatment. A person with terminal cancer can decide when enough is enough and prohibit further surgery or chemotherapy. Any imposition of unwanted treatment will constitute assault, however genuinely his doctors believe that the patient might benefit from continuing treatment. In England at least, no patient has to justify rejecting even life-saving treatment. 'It matters not whether the reasons for refusal were rational, or irrational, unknown or even non-existent[9].' Moreover patients can ensure that they control the stage at which treatment should cease even when that point arrives at a time when they are no longer able to communicate their wishes. Advance directives already have legal force in common law jurisdictions, even where no specific legislation yet exists. Providing there is unequivocal evidence that a certain mode of treatment was prohibited by the patient, it is as much assault to impose that treatment on the now unconscious or incompetent patient as to force similar treatment on an actively protesting individual[10].

In circumstances where refusing further treatment effects a person's wish to die, he enjoys a right to die. However injury or disease may result in disability or suffering the patient finds intolerable, yet life looks set to continue. The terminally ill patient may regard the likely 'natural' termination of her life as too long delayed. Her desire to die encompasses a wish for immediate death, a demand to be killed. If a competent patient freely seeks to exercise such a choice that cannot be violation of his right to life? And what of other fundamental human rights?

The European Convention, albeit it nowhere touches on a right to die, establishes other rights pertinent to the patient who desires to die. No-one may be subjected to torture or to inhuman or degrading treatment or punishment[11]. Does there come a point when continued existence equates to degrading treatment? Is 'life' sustained via tubes feeding you and tubes evacuating bowels and bladder equivalent to torture when imposed on an unwilling patient? Such may well be the case, but the right not to be subjected to degrading treatment does no more than reinforce the right to refuse further or continuing treatment. What of the right to privacy[12]?

Might it be contended that so long as a competent patient who freely makes a choice to die can find a willing accomplice to effect an act that were he capable of carrying out himself would not be criminal, it is an invasion of privacy to interfere with that choice. If suicide is permitted society has accepted the individual's right to choose to end her life. It may seem unjust to deny that right to those so ill or disabled as to be incapable of doing so independently.

In those jurisdictions who as yet refuse to lift the prohibition on active killing, the justification for the consequent denial of choice to the patient is often thought to rest on what has been judicially described as 'society's interest . . . in upholding the concept that all human life is sacred'[13]. Does a doctrine of sanctity of life still command support today? And are there perhaps other, more pragmatic, grounds for the law's unease about active euthanasia?

Sanctity of life or legal pragmatism?

Traditional Judaeo-Christian belief in human life as a gift from a divine creator and thus literally sacred probably no longer commands majority support in the UK at least. Religious practice is a minority pursuit in England. In the absence of an active and universal faith in a divinity does the concept of sanctity of life cease to have any place in the law? If I profess to believe that life is sacred and ends at God's command not mine, that belief mandates I may neither seek my own death nor hasten another's. That faith, it might be argued, no more entitles me to enforce that belief on others than it would justify me in compelling non-believing neighbours to attend Holy Communion to 'save their souls'.

There can be little doubt that Judaeo-Christian concepts of sanctity of life historically played their part in the law's condemnation of active euthanasia and suicide. However, they were far from the sole factor influencing the development of laws on homicide. Preservation of public order and engendering safeguards against the fallibility, and outright evil, inherent in mankind, played their own role. Nor is adherence to sanctity of life an exclusively religious phenomenon. Seamless respect for human life in all its infinite variety is a value espoused by many atheists and agnostics. 'Belief in the special worth of human life is at the heart of all civilised societies[14].' There would be few who would dissent from such a notion. Working out what such fine words mean is quite another matter. The House of Lords Select Committee on Medical Ethics concluded that they outlawed any reform of the law designed to 'weaken society's prohibition of intentional killing[15].' Yet their Lordships did not endorse (or at least not expressly) any concept that God prohibited such a course of action. They offered pragmatic, not theological or philosophical, grounds for maintaining such a ban.

'We do not think it is possible to set secure limits on voluntary euthanasia[16].' 'We are also concerned that vulnerable people...would feel pressure to seek early death[17].' Respect for human life, the right to life, even if it allows for the individual to choose to end that life, still demands that the law ensures no third party usurps the individual's choice. In principle, a right to seek assistance in dying might command recognition in a secular society. In practice, how can abuse by others of such a right be prevented? Choice requires options from which to choose. If hospice care is not available to all terminally ill patients, if standards of palliative care vary, are the necessary options available? Fear of covert compulsion clouds the debate on voluntary euthanasia. In The Netherlands, where the 'great experiment' on euthanasia is now in train, commentators suggest a significant number of patients have their life ended without their express consent. Others express the desire to die but do so out of fear of burdening their families[18]. Hovering in the background too, beyond the boundaries of The Netherlands, is the issue of the cost of health care. If painless death is an option to the terminally or incurably ill, will publicly funded health authorities purchase expensive palliative care for their patients? Will private insurance cover the cost of dying slowly for increasing numbers of sick, very elderly patients?

However, the arguments just advanced are themselves pretty fallible. If it is right in principle to acknowledge a right to choose to be killed, the lawyers must struggle to find appropriate means of enforcing that right. Why should the suffering patient pay the cost of the law's inadequacy? The failure for the most part to confront reform of laws relating to active euthanasia suggests that some lingering notion of a more general doctrine of sanctity of life endures.

De-medicalising euthanasia

The logic of acknowledging a right to an autonomous choice to be killed is this. Legislation need do no more than ensure a means of obtaining unequivocal evidence of the individual's free and informed choice and that appropriate, humane mechanisms exist to effect that choice. A statute could provide as follows. An adult of sound mind should be entitled to request to be killed. That request should be made in front of two witnesses who attest that the request is made voluntarily and on the basis of informed choice. The request must be repeated after a waiting period of 7 days. That period could exceptionally be reduced by leave of the court. A licensed thanatologist (death-bringer) could then lawfully end the person's life in an approved manner. Regulations made under the statute would prescribe (*inter alia*) what information must be made available to the person making the request, what training thanatologists should receive, and what qualifications witnesses must meet. Doctors and nurses would not figure in the picture at all. One of the anxieties expressed about active euthanasia, the 'brutalisation' of caring professionals, is countered. Alex Capron need no longer fear that he will never know whether his doctor approaches his bed wearing the white coat of the healer or the black hood of the executioner[19]. The licensed thanatologist will wear a simple and distinctive uniform!

No voluntary euthanasia proposal I have seen, endorses such a simple scheme. All follow the lead of The Netherlands and medicalise ending life. A doctor must determine that the patient's suffering is intolerable, that he is terminally ill, that other means of alleviating suffering are no longer feasible. A second independent doctor must confirm her colleague's conclusion. Then and only then, doctors may end life. Euthanasia is a medical act performed when doctors judge that a patient's quality of life is none or minimal. The exact pattern may vary but virtually all proponents of voluntary euthanasia, and any proposal for non-voluntary euthanasia, medicalise the process. There is a certain irony in this state of affairs. In a society which contains many members who do not believe in God, a society which vehemently objects to doctors 'playing God', whenever an attempt is made to re-write the script on euthanasia, doctors get cast as God. Perhaps unease at permitting active killing even by purportedly free choice runs deeper than we think.

Covert euthanasia

Critics of the House of Lords Select Committee's inability to endorse active euthanasia because secure limits cannot be set on the practice have one especially powerful weapon at their disposal. It is almost universally conceded that doctors and nurses do occasionally, usually in the privacy of a patient's home, end life. Pain relieving drugs are administered in dosages that will be more than likely to hasten death. The doctrine of 'double effect' endorsed in *R vs Adams*[20] can only tenuously be advanced to justify what is done as designed to relieve suffering and only incidentally hastening death. Covert euthanasia happens. It is carried out without any provisos for explicit request on the part of the patient. It is unregulated and so susceptible to all the potential abuses which are supposed to rule out regulated euthanasia. The law must be an ass to condone what it cannot bring itself to permit?

The question which must be asked by doctors before they gleefully agree with that proposition is simple, if brutal. If a particular society cannot achieve consensus on the nature of human life, if a society concurs that even if it might accept voluntary euthanasia, strict safeguards must reinforce respect for human life, by what means can the law most effectively provide such safeguards? Can the boundary between an act of humanely ending suffering and an act manifesting disregard for the value of life be better policed than by the knowledge that crossing the boundary attracts a conviction for homicide? Could any other sanction better signal the responsibility the law attaches to 'playing God'? 'Unfair to doctors' would be a predictable response. Why should a professional act at peril of her liberty or risk depriving her patient of an ultimate manifestation of professional care? Maybe one rejoinder might be that unsatisfactory, even irrational, though the current law may seem, at least it usually keeps lawyers away from the death bed. Regulating, formalising, active euthanasia when a significant number of professionals and laypersons deplore such a move will have one certain result. The law will interfere more not less in the final stages of the professional's relationship with his patient.

Acknowledgements

I would like to thank my colleague at Manchester, Professor Stuart Donnan, Professor of Public Health and Epidemiology, for introducing me to the novel concept of a profession of thanatologist.

References

1 See Mason JK, McCall Smith RA. *Law and medical ethics* 4th edn. London: Butterworths 1994: pp 316–7
2 Article 2(1) of the *European Convention for the Protection of Human Rights and Fundamental Freedoms*
3 *Abortion Act 1967* section 1(1)(d) as amended by section 37 of the *Human Fertilisation and Embryology Act 1990*; see Brazier M. *Medicine, patients and the law* 2nd edn. London: Penguin 1992: pp 302–4
4 R vs Cambridge Health Authority ex p B. *All Engl Rep&D 1995*; **2**: 129
5 Re C (a minor) (wardship: medical treatment). *All Engl Rep* 1989; **2**: 82
6 Re J (a minor) (wardship: medical treatment). *All Engl Rep* 1990; **3**: 930
7 At p 938 per Lord Donaldson MR
8 Airedale NHS Trust vs Bland. *All Engl Rep* 1993; **1**: 821
9 Re T (adult: refusal of medical treatment). *All Engl Rep* 1992; **4** 649, at p 664 per Lord Donaldson MR
10 Re T (above); Re C (refusal of medical treatment) *All Engl Rep* 1994; **1** 819; Malette vs Shulman. *Dominion Law Rep* (4th) 1990; **67** 321. See also Law Commission Report No. 231

Mental incapacity. London: HMSO 1995, recommending granting statutory force to advance directives

11 Article 3

12 Article 8. A number of judgments expressly seek to balance respect for the right to life with a right to 'human dignity'; see Airedale NHS Trust vs Bland. *All Engl Rep* 1993; **1**: 821 at p. 855 per Hoffmann LJ. in the English Court of Appeal; Rodriguez vs A-G of British Columbia. *WWR* 1993; **3**: 553, per Cory J in the Canadian Supreme Court

13 Re T (above) at p 661 per Lord Donaldson MR. See generally, Kennedy I, Grubb A. *Medical law – text with materials*. 2nd edn. London: Butterworths, 1994: pp 1197–9

14 *Report of the Select Committee of Medical Ethics* HL 21-1. London: HMS0, 1993: para 34

15 &I:op cit&D: see para 237

16 &I:op cit&D: at para 238

17 &I:op cit&D: at para 239

18 See Keown J. The law and practice of euthanasia in The Netherlands. *Law Q Rev* 1992; **108**: 51

19 Capron AM. Legal and ethical problems in decisions for death. *Law Med Health Care* 1986; **14** 141

20 *Criminal Law Rev* 1957; 365; see generally Brazier M. *op. cit.* at pp 446–7.

Euthanasia: law and practice in The Netherlands

Sjef Gevers

Health Law Section, University of Amsterdam, Amsterdam, The Netherlands

In The Netherlands, euthanasia is defined as the deliberate termination of the life of a person on his request by another person. Although, in this limited sense, euthanasia is only one of the issues raised by medical decision-making at the end of life, it is, in particular, the acceptance of euthanasia in this country that has attracted attention from abroad. Also, in The Netherlands itself, the toleration of the courts of euthanasia (if carried out by a physician under strict conditions) has given rise to much debate. This contribution surveys the developments in the law (including recent legislation), and in medical practice, and explores the relation between the two, with particular attention to the position of the physician.

Usually, 'euthanasia' is defined in a broad sense, encompassing all decisions (of doctors or others) intended to hasten or to bring about the death of a person (by act or omission) in order to prevent or to limit the suffering of that person (whether or not on his or her request). In The Netherlands, the word has a more limited meaning; it only refers to the deliberate termination of the life of a person on his request by another person (i.e. active, voluntary euthanasia)[1]. This contribution deals with the regulation and practice of euthanasia in this limited sense. It is also in this sense that euthanasia in The Netherlands has attracted so much attention and raised so much controversy.

This is not to say, of course, that euthanasia is necessarily the most important, let alone the only, issue as far as medical decisions relating to the end of life are concerned. Due to an aging population, sociocultural developments and the increasing potential of medical technology to prolong life, physicians (in The Netherlands and elsewhere) have increasingly to face difficult dilemmas, first of all on whether or not to withhold (or refrain from) treatment. Also in The Netherlands (as in Britain, the USA, and other countries) there is much discussion on non-treatment decisions, in particular when incompetent patients (severely handicapped newborns, comatose patients, patients with sever dementia, or others) are concerned.

With regard to these decisions, however, the situation in The Netherlands would not seem to be basically at variance with accepted practice in most other countries. Therefore, this contribution will focus on (active, voluntary) euthanasia. It will deal first of all with the role of

Postal address:
Prof Dr JKM Gevers,
Institute of Social Medi-
cine, Academic Medical
Center, Meibergdreef 15
1105 AZ Amsterdam,
The Netherlands

the courts and the profession in the regulation of euthanasia. Subsequently, medical practice will be discussed, with particular reference to recent empirical studies conducted in this field. Finally, an account will be given of the development of the notification procedure, of legislation and of prosecution policies.

The development of law

According to the Dutch Penal Code, euthanasia is a crime. However, it is not qualified as murder (as in some other countries), but dealt with in a separate section: according to Article 293, anyone who takes another person's life at his explicit and earnest request will be punished by imprisonment to a maximum of 12 years.

The Dutch debate on euthanasia was sparked by a court case in 1973 (the same year in which the Dutch Society for Voluntary Euthanasia was formed). In this case, a general practitioner was prosecuted for ending the life of her mother, who had suffered a cerebral haemorrhage, was partly paralysed, was deaf, and had trouble speaking. After the mother had repeatedly expressed the wish to die, the daughter ended her mother's life by giving her a lethal dose of morphine. The court (of Leeuwarden) found her guilty, not because she had hastened the death of her mother (who was incurably ill and suffered unbearably), but because she had directly ended her life instead of stepping up the doses of morphia with the secondary effect that the patient's life would have been shortened. The court gave her a suspended sentence of one week imprisonment and put her on probation for a year. In later decisions, the courts no longer exclude that a doctor may bring about the death of the patient in a direct way, but they have elaborated the criteria developed in the Leeuwarden decision and added other requirements.

Of the many other court rulings over the last two decades, I will only discuss the case which resulted in the landmark decision of the Supreme Court in 1984. This case (known as the Alkmaar case) concerned a 95-year-old woman who was seriously ill with no chance of recovery. The weekend before her death, she suffered substantial deterioration, was unable to eat or drink, and lost consciousness. She had pleaded with the doctor several times to put an end to her agony. After regaining consciousness, she declared that she did not want to go through such an experience again and urged her physician to end her life. Finally, the doctor decided to act according to her wishes as he was convinced that every single day would only be a heavy burden to the patient.

Doctors prosecuted for euthanasia have defended themselves in different ways. The only plea for acquittal which was not dismissed, and which was also accepted by the Supreme Court in 1984, is the invocation of a situation of 'force majeure' (or necessity), resulting from a conflict of duties: the duty towards the patient to alleviate hopeless suffering and the duty towards the law to preserve the patient's life. A doctor will not be convicted if he or she has carefully balanced the conflicting duties and made a decision that can objectively be justified, taking into account the special circumstances of the case.

According to the Supreme Court in the Alkmaar case, the Court of Appeals of Amsterdam had not given sufficient reasons for its conviction of the doctor; in particular, it should have investigated whether, according to responsible medical opinion, a necessity (conflict of duties) had existed. In doing so, it should have taken into account, for instance, whether it could be expected that the patient would soon no longer be able to die with dignity in circumstances worthy of a human being. The case was referred to the Court of The Hague, which acquitted the doctor. In the same year, the Royal Dutch Medical Association issued an influential statement on euthanasia. While acknowledging the fact that in a pluralistic society there would never be consensus on matters such as abortion and euthanasia, including among doctors, the medical association stated that euthanasia might be acceptable in certain circumstances. In order to provide guidance to the profession as to under which conditions euthanasia could be permissible, it formulated a set of criteria that mirror the criteria developed by the courts:

- the request for euthanasia must come from the patient and be entirely free and voluntary, well considered and persistent
- the patient must experience intolerable suffering (physical or mental), with no prospect of improvement and with no acceptable solutions to alleviate the patient's situation
- euthanasia must be performed by a physician after consultation with an independent colleague who has experience in this field[2]

A year later (1985), the State Commission on Euthanasia (established in 1982 to advise the Government on its future policy with regard to legislation) proposed that Article 293 or the Penal Code be amended in such a way that the intentional termination of another person's life at the latter's express and earnest request would not be an offence, provided this is carried out by a doctor in the context of careful medical practice in respect of a patient who is in an untenable situation with no prospect of improvement[3]. As will be explained below, that proposal has never resulted in a amendment of the Penal Code.

In applying the aforementioned criteria, several other questions have been addressed by the courts in subsequent decisions. I will briefly comment on two of them.

Court decisions do not exclude the possibility that the patient's request is laid down in an advance directive drawn up by the patient while still competent. However, it is obvious that, in such a case, great caution is required, for instance with regard to the situation to which the statement is meant to apply. Until now, only one such case has been before a disciplinary court; in 1994, the Central Medical Disciplinary Court apparently accepted the written statement as a valid request. In a recent report on patients with severe dementia (1993), a commission of the Dutch Medical Association expressed strong reservations concerning euthanasia on the basis of such an advance directive at least as far as patients with dementia are concerned.

The courts do not require that the patient is terminally ill and that his death is imminent (see, for instance, the decision of the Court of The Hague in 1985, which acquitted an anaesthesiologist who had administered euthanasia on the request of a very ill patient suffering from multiple sclerosis). But if this is not the case, the physician will have to do more in explaining why the patient was in an untenable situation and why acceptable alternatives were not available. The same applies when the patient's suffering is of a psychological rather than of a physical nature (see also the Supreme Court decision of 21 June 1994 – Chabot case – on assistance in suicide of a mental patient).

Medical practice

The pattern of court decisions and the positions taken by the Dutch Medical Association and the State Commission of 1985, have facilitated an open discussion of medical practice in this field, both in medical journals and in the public press. Nevertheless, it has taken some time before more precise data on the practice of euthanasia became available.

The most extensive and important study was conducted under the auspices of an official committee of inquiry (Remmelink committee) set up by the Dutch Government in 1990; in September 1991, the committee published its report which included data not only on euthanasia, but also on other medical decisions concerning the end of life, such as withholding or withdrawing of treatment[4]. In the past, estimated numbers of cases of euthanasia had ranged between 2,000 and 8,000 a year. This study found 2,300 cases in 1990, which amounts to about 1.8% of the 129,000 deaths in The Netherlands in that year. Furthermore, 400 cases of physician assisted suicide were reported. Another study, published a year later and also based on self reports of doctors obtained in strict anonymity, yielded similar results and confirmed also most of the other findings of the Remmelink report[5].

The number of initial requests for euthanasia or assisted suicide was around 3 times as high as the number of cases in which it actually took place. Obviously, in many cases alternatives are found, patients change their mind or die naturally, or the doctor turns down their request. Requests were made by patients for reasons of loss of dignity (mentioned in 57% of cases), pain (46%), being dependent on others (33%), or tiredness of life (23%); only in 6% was pain the only reason. When euthanasia was performed, life was shortened by at least 1 week in 70% of all cases, and in 8% by more than 6 months. In these cases, cancer was especially prominent (68% as opposed to 27% for all deaths).

One of the findings of the study, which has attracted much attention (in The Netherlands and abroad), is that in about 1,000 cases (0.8% of all deaths), doctors prescribed or administered a drug with the objective of shortening the life of the patient, without the latter's explicit request. In the large majority of these cases, death was imminent; in most cases, patients were in the end stage of a malignant disease and were dying; in almost all cases patients were suffering grievously. Most patients were incompetent at the time of the decision, but, in more than half of the cases, it had been discussed with him or her while still competent. These cases do not meet the strict criteria for euthanasia developed in jurisprudence. I refer to them because they have played an important role in the legal developments of the last few years (see below).

Euthanasia would seem to occur much more often in general practice than in hospitals (euthanasia in nursing homes is rare). According to a report published in 1994, euthanasia or assisted suicide is performed as much as 3 times more often by general practitioners than by other physicians. To a large extent, this can be explained by the generally long-standing relationship between the patient and his or her physician in general practice[6].

Notification and prosecution

Under Dutch law, a physician can only issue a death certificate in the case of natural death; in other cases he has to notify the municipal medical examiner, who, after investigating the case, will report to the public prosecutor, that is the district attorney. Until 1990, this would frequently result in a police investigation; these investigations could be very burdensome for physicians and the police would often not limit themselves to interrogating the doctor. From 1982 onwards, reported cases were discussed at national level in the meetings of the attorneys general. They would decide on whether or not the physician in question would be prosecuted.

Before 1985, doctors usually did not report euthanasia. After several doctors had been convicted by the courts for writing a false death certificate, the number of reported cases of euthanasia started to increase. In 1989, 338 cases were officially registered, which is less, however, than 20% of the estimated total number in that year. Many doctors felt they were being unjustly criminalised by the existing notification procedure. Whereas, in some districts, agreements between the public prosecution and local physicians would result in respectful treatment, in other districts police officers would come close to arresting the physician[7].

In 1990, a new procedure was agreed upon by the Minister of Justice and the Royal Dutch Medical Association, which argued that a less deterrent procedure would be much more effective. In entering into this official agreement, the Dutch Government took a small, but significant, step in the direction of not only tolerating, but also decriminalising the practice of euthanasia. That it was willing to do so cannot only be explained by the pressure exerted on it by the medical profession, but also by the fact that it needed the support and cooperation of the profession in conducting the nationwide study described in the preceding section.

The new procedure is as follows. The physician informs the local medical examiner by means of an extensive questionnaire; the medical examiner then reports to the district attorney. When he is satisfied that the criteria laid down by the courts are complied with, the public prosecutor will issue a certificate of no objection to burial or cremation; in other cases, he may order an investigation and decide to prosecute the case.

Since this procedure came into force, the number of reported cases has increased dramatically: from 454 in 1990, to 1,424 in 1994 (which is about 50% of the estimated total number of cases of euthanasia and assisted suicide). At the same time, the percentage of prosecutions has decreased. Whereas, in 1983, proceedings were instituted in two out of the ten cases reported in that year, in 1992, four cases were prosecuted only out of the total number of 1,322 reported cases. One may be tempted to conclude, that the unreported cases do not meet the standards; research indicates, however, that most of these cases meet the substantive requirements developed by the courts[8].

The question whether the Penal Code (Article 293) should be changed to bring existing legislation more in accordance with medical practice has been a matter of extensive debate for many years[9]. Reference has already been made to the proposals of the State Commission in 1985 (see above). From 1984 onwards, various bills were introduced into Parliament but none was adopted. After receiving (in 1991) the results of the study on medical decisions concerning the end of life, the Government submitted a new proposal to Parliament which would modify existing legislation be it to a very limited extent. According to the Bill, Article 293 would not be changed, but the notification procedure agreed upon in 1990 would be laid down in regulations under the Burial Act and thereby acquire formal legal status. At the same time – in particular, in reaction to the finding of 1,000 cases in which doctors would have shortened the life of patients without their explicit request – its scope would be extended: it would also apply to doctors ending the life of a patient without his or her request.

In particular, the latter element has been criticised: it would wrongly suggest that cases, in which there is no previous, unambiguous request, can be dealt with on the same basis as cases of euthanasia. In the parliamentary debate on the Bill, the Government has repeated time and again, however, that, in principle, such cases would be prosecuted. On the other hand, when the substantive requirements developed by the courts are met, in general no proceedings will be instituted. The Government also made it clear, however, that a doctor performing euthanasia would never be completely immune from criminal prosecution.

On the whole, the position taken by the Government would seem ambiguous: euthanasia will remain a crime even if it is carried out by a doctor who complies with all the restrictions elaborated in the court rulings. But at the same time, the modification of the Burial Act implies that a doctor will not be prosecuted if he or she carefully commits that crime. After long discussions in Parliament, the Bill was adopted; although quite a few Members of Parliament were not satisfied with the outcome of the debate, it turned out impossible to find a majority which would support a more straight-forward proposal. The new law came into force on 1 June 1994.

Conclusions

If one not only looks at the legislation, but tries to strike a more general balance of developments in The Netherlands, the following can be observed. Although euthanasia is by no means universally accepted in The Netherlands, there would seem to be less controversy over the present policy than there has been in the years before. A delicate balance has been achieved between statutory law that prohibits euthanasia, case law that stipulates conditions for non-prosecution, and controlled acceptance in practice. Empirical data are available on what doctors do, both in general practice and in hospitals. Orderly reporting has increased considerably. Some (like the Royal Dutch Medical Association) would prefer further legislation, mainly to enhance legal certainty for physicians performing euthanasia. Others are of the opinion that the complicated issues of medical decision-making at the end of life elude attempts at legislation; such attempts would only result in political conflict or in unsatisfactory compromise.

The discovery of cases of ending of life without an explicit request is a matter of grave concern, but even that has a positive side: it makes it possible to address this issue and to reduce the number of such cases as far as possible[10]. The existence of these cases does not necessarily demonstrate that the Dutch are skiing down the 'slippery slope': we do not know whether these cases also occurred before euthanasia was openly accepted. Nor do we know to what extent doctors in other countries shorten the lives of desperately ill patients, with or without their explicit involvement[11].

If, in the future, other countries also leave some room for euthanasia, they will have to face similar problems as those which emerged in The Netherlands. In the solutions to these problems there will be differences from one country to another. One should be careful in transferring the Dutch experience to other countries. The delicate balance between prohibition and acceptance mentioned before cannot be completely disconnected from the social structure of Dutch society, the legal system and the cultural climate on the one hand, and the system of health care and insurance on the other[12].

References

1 Dillman RJM, Legemaate J. Euthanasia in The Netherlands; the state of the debate. &I:Eur J Health Law 1994; **1**: 81–7
2 Borst-Eilers E. Euthanasia in The Netherlands: brief historical review and present situation. In: Misbin RI. ed. *Euthanasia: the good of the patient, the good of society.* Frederick: University Publishing, 1992: 55–68
3 Final report of The Netherland's State Commission on euthanasia: an English summary. *Bioethics* 1987; **1**: 163-74
4 Van der Maas PJ, Van Delden JJM, Pijnenborg L, Looman CWN. Euthanasia and other medical decisions concerning the end of life. *Lancet* 1991; **338**: 669–74
5 Van der Wal G, Van Eijk JTM, Leenen HJJ, Spreeuwenberg C. Euthanasia and assisted suicide. *Fam Pract* 1992; **9**: 130–4
6 Pijnenborg L, Van Delden JJM, Kardaun JWPF, Glerum JJ, Van der Maas PJ. Nationwide study of decisions concerning the end of life in general practice in The Netherlands. *BMJ* 1994; **309**: 1209–12
7 Van Delden JJM, Pijnenborg P, Van der Maas PJ. The Remmelink study; two years later. *Hastings Cent Rep* 1993; **Nov–Dec**: 24–7
8 Van der Wal G. *Euthanasia and assisted suicide by family doctors.* Rotterdam: WYT Uitgeefgroep, 1992 (in Dutch, English summary)
9 Gevers JKM. Legislation on euthanasia: recent developments in The Netherlands. *J Med Ethics* 1992; **18**: 138–41
10 Van der Wal G, Dillman RJM. Euthanasia in The Netherlands. *BMJ* 1994; **308**: 1346–9
11 Kuhse H, Singer P. From the editors. *Bioethics* 1992; **6(4)**: iii-vi
12 Pabst Battin M. Should we copy the Dutch? The Netherlands' practice of voluntary active euthanasia as a model for the United States. In: Misbin RI. ed. *Euthanasia: the good of the patient, the good of society.* Frederick: University Publishing, 1992: 95–103

Euthanasia: the law in the United Kingdom

Alexander McCall Smith

Faculty of Law, University of Edinburgh, Edinburgh, UK

The regulation of euthanasia by the criminal law has tended to be one of the more contentious areas of medical law, and continues to be the subject of debate. Few areas of the criminal law have been so consistently the target of reformist pressure, and certainly few areas have so strongly resisted change. Understandably, legislators are unwilling to involve themselves in a matter of law reform which engenders such moral disagreement, and it is significant that only two jurisdictions – The Netherlands and the Australian Northern Territories – have made any substantial change in their legal practice in this area. In other countries, including the UK, the courts and legislators have consistently refused to remove the fundamental criminal law objection to the practice of euthanasia. This is not to say, of course, that the courts have failed to recognise the medical subtleties in medical treatment at the end of life; in several important decisions, the courts in Britain have considered the boundaries of the criminal law's protection of life and have offered guidelines for doctors facing the delicate issues associated with treating the dying patient. Yet, in spite of several helpful decisions from the courts, the basic principle remains firm: the criminal law does not countenance the taking of life, no matter how good the motive. This means that there are very clear legal limits to the extent to which doctors can follow their individual consciences in this area.

Direct acts of euthanasia

The criminal law regards as a potential offence of homicide any wrongful act which results in the loss of life. Such an act may be intended to lead to the death of another, or it may result from negligence, recklessness, or a culpable omission. The most serious homicide offence is murder, which in Britain involves a mandatory penalty of life imprisonment. Manslaughter (culpable homicide in Scotland) is less serious and will often attract a much less stringent penalty – in some cases no more than a relatively short term of imprisonment or other minor sanction.

When life is taken deliberately, the appropriate charge is murder. Thus, if a doctor responds to a request from a patient to end his life and administers a lethal injection, the doctor will have acted with the necessary *mens rea* for murder (*mens rea* is the mental element required

*Postal address:
Dr A McCall Smith,
Faculty of Law, University
of Edinburgh, South
Bridge, Edinburgh
EH8 9YL, UK*

for conviction of a crime). It makes no difference from the legal point of view that the patient gave his consent to the doctor's act. Consent is no defence to a charge of murder, or indeed to the infliction of any substantial physical injury on another. Nor does the doctor's motive make any difference; the fact that this was a case of 'mercy killing' does not affect the status of the act as one of murder.

The prosecution of doctors for acts of euthanasia is rare, but there have been several cases in which the medical profession has been reminded of the law's determination to protect human life. In the two best-known earlier cases, that of Dr John Bodkin Adams[1], and that of Dr Leonard Arthur[2], the issue was complicated by the fact that one involved the administration of pain killers for which there was medical justification, and the other involved the withholding of treatment. More recently, however, in the case of Dr Cox[3], the legal point was more focused. Dr Cox was convicted of the attempted murder of a patient to whom he had administered a lethal injection of potassium chloride. But for the technical reasons which restricted the charge to one of attempted murder, Dr Cox might have found himself faced with the more serious charge of murder, although it is far from certain what the outcome of such a charge might have been. The point which his conviction makes, though, is that juries are prepared to convict doctors who engage in consensual euthanasia, even in circumstances where a great deal of sympathy might be felt for the doctor. Dr Cox had treated his patient for some time and was sensitive to her suffering; his mistake, though, may have been to assume that acting in good faith and in accordance with the promptings of conscience would protect him from the rigours of the criminal law.

There are, of course, ways in which the severity of the criminal law can be mitigated, even where the act in question is one of intentional killing. In those cases where a relative or other person caring for a patient in extreme distress takes the patient's life, then a successful plea of diminished responsibility may reduce the charge from murder to the lesser charge of manslaughter (or culpable homicide). This can be done where there is medical evidence that the person who took life was suffering from a psychiatric illness at the time of the act. A reactive depression, brought about by the distress of caring for the dying relative, would clearly meet this requirement. Such a plea, however, is unlikely to be available to a doctor or nurse.

Indirect or 'passive' euthanasia

The administration of a fatal dose of drugs may not be necessary to achieve the goal of bringing a patient's life to an end. A decision to refrain from embarking on a course of treatment, or a decision to withdraw a treatment already in progress, may have the effect of ending life, just as surely as the injection of a lethal substance. Such decisions are made regularly, and are an inevitable part of the humane and conscientious practice of medicine. They are strongly, and convincingly, defended by doctors, and indeed it has been pointed out by one paediatrician that such decisions are incorrectly called 'the withdrawal of treatment'; on the contrary, they constitute, in themselves, an integral part of the medical treatment of the dying patient[4].

The criminal law does not require doctors to persist in the treatment of a patient when no medical purpose is served by such persistence. All that is required, from the legal point of view, is that the patient be given such treatment as is medically appropriate in the circumstances. Deciding what is medically appropriate is clearly crucial. A decision to deny antibiotics to a young and otherwise healthy patient with a chest infection is quite a different matter from a decision not to treat a similar condition in an elderly patient with a very poor quality of life and a poor prognosis. In the former case, the withholding of treatment is potentially criminally culpable; in the latter, the law accepts that the limits of medical duty have been reached and there may be no further obligation to provide more than treatment which makes the patient comfortable. Such a view accords with our common sense of human limitation and our distaste for the vain pursuit of longevity beyond the natural measure.

Uncertainty about the circumstances in which it is proper to refrain from further treatment, or to limit treatment, has been considerably diminished in English law in a series of court decisions concerning infants. The two most important of these were the cases of *Re C*[5] and *Re J*[6]. In the first of these cases, *Re C*, the infant was moribund and the hospital sought authority to abstain from the setting up of naso-gastric feeding or the administration of antibiotics should either of these become necessary. The court confirmed that this was quite proper and that all that would be required was that the patient should be made comfortable and allowed to die with peace and dignity. By contrast, the child in *Re J* was not dying. He was severely brain-damaged and suffered from fits during which he required assistance in breathing. The court ruled that there was no hard and fast legal requirement that in such a case the child should be resuscitated; the decision was one for the doctors and parents to make in consultation with one another and with the child's best interests as the main consideration. In deciding what was in the child's best interests, the matter should be looked at from the point of view of what might be assumed to be the patient's point of view, and in this the issue of pain and suffering fell to be considered. At the same time, however, the court stressed that it was not authorising euthanasia. As the judge said:

The court never sanctions steps to terminate life. That would be unlawful. There is no question of approving, even in the case of the most horrendous disability, a course aimed at terminating life or accelerating death. The court is concerned only with the circumstances in which steps should not be taken to prolong life[7].

These cases were concerned with patients who could not express their own wishes on the subject of their treatment. An unconscious or incapacitated adult might be in the same position, although in the case of an adult there might be evidence of what the patient's previously-expressed views were. If it is the case that the patient has previously stated that he does not wish to be subjected to a particular form of treatment, then this evidence should weigh very heavily with a court. At present there are no decisions by UK courts in which the validity of advance directives (so-called 'living wills') is specifically ruled upon, but several judicial comments demonstrate a sympathetic attitude towards such statements of preference[8]. In one case involving a mentally disordered patient, the court held that the surgery should not be performed on a man who, while still mentally competent, had expressed his antipathy to the such an operation[9]. This case could be taken to indicate an acceptance of the advance directive, and it is likely that if a case comes before a British court in which the validity of a directive against treatment is considered, the directive will be upheld. The crucial matter, however, will be the question of whether the earlier statement can be taken to embody the current view of the patient. Clearly this is the major drawback with advance directives; people can change their opinions, and a view expressed while in good health may not represent what is wanted by one who is facing death.

A further objection to the concept of the advance directive is that it potentially limits the extent to which the doctor can use his own judgement to assess the needs of the patient in the context of the family. It may sometimes be necessary to carry out a subtle balancing of the interests of the patient and the family. It may mean a great deal to family members that the patient's life be prolonged or that a particular treatment be attempted. Although ultimately it must be recognised that the patient's autonomy, or right of self-determination, must be the deciding factor, this can be combined with a recognition of family feelings and a compromise between the patient's known wishes and family desires might be achieved. In any event, a process of sympathetic discussion and sensitive accommodation of family wishes might be achieved more readily by a doctor who feels that he does not have his hands tied by the strict terms of a legal document that must be applied to the letter. The weight of this objection, however, is questionable, and in so far as there is a consensus of legal opinion on this matter, it undoubtedly favours giving effect wherever possible to the patient's previously expressed preferences.

Withdrawal of nutrition and hydration

A particularly difficult problem is posed by those unconscious patients who are dependent on artificial feeding for their survival. While there may be no duty to persist with medical treatment past the point at which such treatment serves any useful purpose, there is a clear continuing obligation to provide for the basic needs of the patient. This has usually been taken to mean that the provision of essential nursing care – including the provision of food and water – is legally required until such time as death intervenes.

In the case of a patient who is capable of swallowing, this requirement poses no difficulties; such a patient must be given food and water even if medical interventions are abandoned. A patient in the persistent vegetative state (PVS) may, however, require nutrition and hydration by tube and may, therefore, be both irretrievably unconscious and entirely reliant on artificial methods for the provision of the necessities of life. Clinically such a person may not be diagnosed as brain dead because sufficient brain stem function remains to sustain spontaneous breathing and circulation: but the two states are similar in that in neither is there evidence of awareness, of any sort, and both are considered irreversible.

Litigation in England has now clarified the position of such patients, at least as far as civil law matters are concerned. In *Airedale National Health Service Trust vs Bland*[10], the House of Lords considered the position of a young man who had suffered severe brain injury in a football stadium disaster and who had entered into the persistent vegetative state. It was accepted by the patient's doctors and parents alike that there was no prospect of the recovery of consciousness and in these circumstances the hospital sought legal permission to withdraw the naso-gastric feeding regime in order to allow the patient to die.

The resulting judgments, both at the Court of Appeal stage and in the House of Lords, are models of the sensitive legal treatment of an emotionally-charged issue and have met with broad, if not unanimous, approval. At their heart lay a view of the provision artificial feeding as an aspect of medical treatment rather than as a distinct duty. Once this was done, then the decision whether or not to continue with it could be resolved in exactly the same way as any other treatment decision, and for this purpose the 'best interests' test could be invoked. Was it in the best interests of Anthony Bland that his body be kept alive when his essential personality and humanity had been destroyed? The court answered no to this question, and the patient, as a result, was allowed to die. Once again, euthanasia had not been authorised, but a clear signal was given that human life need not be maintained at all costs when no possible conscious enjoyment or value could result from such efforts[11].

Courts in other Commonwealth countries have taken a very similar approach to the type of problem considered in *Bland*. In New Zealand, a court authorised the withdrawal of artificial ventilation in the case of a patient suffering from the Guillain-Barré syndrome, on the grounds, amongst others, that artificial ventilation did not amount to a necessity of life where it could only defer certain death. In such a case, the court held, the **manifestations** of life are being preserved rather than life itself[12]. The Canadian courts have also considered the matter, most notably in the *Nancy B vs Hotel-Dieu de Québec*[13], in which the court ruled on the right of another Guillain-Barré sufferer to request, whilst still competent, the withdrawal of respirator treatment.

Assisted suicide

If the criminal law is so rigid in its condemnation of the taking of any active step to end life, then can this legal obstacle be side-stepped by the provision of medical assistance to enable the patient to take his own life? The legal resolution of this depends on the nature of the assistance given, and the circumstances of the individual case. In England, suicide was a crime until the passage of the Suicide Act 1961. This legislation decriminalised suicide (which could obviously only be prosecuted as an attempted crime), but retained the criminal prohibition of aiding and abetting suicide. This means that a doctor who responds to a direct request of a patient to prescribe drugs which he knows the patient intends to use to take his life will be committing an offence under this statute. The position of one who offers advice to another on how to commit suicide is less clear-cut. The matter was considered in *Attorney-General vs Able*[14] in which the court expressed the view that the provision of such advice could constitute aiding and abetting suicide if it was sufficiently closely linked to the act of self-destruction. This view of the law successfully inhibited proponents of voluntary euthanasia in England from openly distributing booklets containing advice on methods of taking one's own life, but did not prevent the Voluntary Euthanasia Society of Scotland from accepting a considerable number of English members, to whom the Scottish Society's booklet was then sent.

The legality of offering such advice in Scotland is even less clear than in England. It is certainly the case that suicide has not been a crime in Scotland – at least in modern times – and, therefore, it is difficult to see how there could be a conviction for being art and part guilty (the Scottish term for accomplice liability) to a non-existent crime. This does not preclude, however, charging a person who assists suicide with a common law crime, such as that of recklessly endangering life. This could even form the basis of a charge of culpable homicide, but whether such a charge, or any charge at all, would be brought in such circumstances would depend on prosecutorial discretion. It is clear, though, that Scots law is far from settled in this area. In practice, exponents of voluntary euthanasia in Scotland distribute their advice booklet responsibly and have not been faced with prosecution. Even in England, where the law is less opaque on this matter, a book published by an American euthanasia reform society is available in bookshops and has not been the subject of prosecution. Successful prosecution would depend, however, on establishing a clear link between the provision of the advice and the act of suicide; something which might be difficult to establish

References

1 For an account of this trial, see Devlin P. *Easing the passing*. London: Bodley Head, 1985
2 &I:The Times 6 November 1981; p 1, 12
3 R. vs Cox *Butterworths Medical Law Reports* 1992; **12**: 38
4 Laing I. Withdrawing from invasive neonatal intensive care. In: Mason JK. ed. *Paediatric forensic medicine and pathology*. London: Chapman and Hall, 1989
5 Re C (a minor) (wardship: medical treatment). *All England Law Reports* 1989; **2**: 782
6 Re J (a minor: wardship: medical treatment). *All England Law Reports* 1990; **3**: 930
7 Note 2 supra at p 943
8 For example, such views were expressed in the House of Lords decision in Airedale National Health Service Trust vs Bland. *All England Law Reports* 1993; **1**: 821
9 Re C (adult refusal of treatment). *All England Law Reports* 1994; **1**: 819
10 *All England Law Reports* 1993; **1**: 821
11 The decision in Bland was followed by a further PVS case: Frenchay NHS Health Trust vs S. 1994
12 Aukland Area Health Board vs Attorney-General. *New Zealand Law Reports* 1993; **1**: 235
13 *Dominion Law Reports* (4th) 1992; **86**: 385
14 *All England Law Reports* 1984; **1**: 277

Towards the right to be killed?

Treatment refusal, assisted suicide and euthanasia in the United States and Canada

Trudo Lemmens

Centre de Recherche en Droit Public, Université de Montréal, Montréal, Québec, Canada

This chapter describes some dominant trends of American and Canadian law in relation to treatment refusal, physician-assisted suicide and euthanasia. Although common law in both countries recognizes the right of patients to refuse treatment, problems have arisen, especially in the US, over treatment refusal on behalf of incompetent patients. One response has been to enact advance-directive legislation, promoting the use of living wills and proxy appointments. Courts have also specified criteria for withholding and withdrawing treatment from incompetent patients. The notion of a 'right to die', developed in court cases on treatment refusal, is now being invoked to support the legalization of assisted suicide. Courts are generally reluctant to recognize an extention of this right. Debates and court cases following the recent initiative to legalize assisted suicide in Oregon and the Sue Rodriguez case in Canada's Supreme Court, which resulted in a special report of a Canadian Senate Committee, are of major importance for the development of law in this area.

Postal address:
M T Lemmens, Centre de Recherche en Droit Public, Université de Montréal, C.P. 6128, Succ. Centre Ville, Montréal, Québec H3C 3J7 Canada

The recent abundance of conflicting lawsuits, legislative initiatives and legal-ethical literature on end-of-life decisions indicate how fiercely Americans are divided on the issue of medical involvement in death. This chapter deals with two aspects: (1) treatment refusal; and (2) physician-assisted suicide and euthanasia. The distinction between these two issues is generally made by courts and in jurisprudence. Legal disputes surrounding end-of-life decisions focused originally on treatment refusal; trendy notions such as 'the right to die', now invoked to defend assisted suicide and euthanasia, were developed in that context. A sound discussion of assisted suicide and euthanasia requires some basic knowledge about the law on withholding or withdrawing treatment. Too often, it is argued that the law actually 'forces' terminally ill or vegetative patients to continue life or even 'causes' unbearable suffering[1]. Polls in the US and Canada indicate that a majority in both countries support assisted suicide and euthanasia. But are they really informed about the current state of the law in relation to treatment refusal? This chapter provides some basic information on the law in the US and in Canada.

Treatment refusal, assisted suicide and euthanasia under American law

Withholding and withdrawing treatment

The right to refuse treatment under common law and constitutional law American common law recognizes that every patient possesses the right of bodily self-determination. In the 1985 Conroy case, the New Jersey Supreme Court described the right of possession of and control over one's body as the most 'sacred right' guarded by common law[2]. This right has been linked with the common-law doctrine of informed consent. Physicians who impose medical treatments without the consent of patients commit the tort of battery. Under common law, therefore, patients are clearly empowered to refuse medical treatment – even when such treatment might save their lives[3,4]. The existence of a constitutional right to refuse treatment is less clear. In earlier cases, it was often argued that both federal and state constitutions protected the right to privacy and that this right included the right to refuse medical treatment. In 1990, in *Cruzan vs Director, Missouri Department of Health*[5], however, the US Supreme Court rejected this point of view. For the sake of argument alone, the Court stated that if there were a constitutional basis for the right to refuse treatment, it would have to be found under the fourteenth amendment's 'liberty interest'. Even though it thus questioned the constitutional character of this right[6-8], some still invoke the Cruzan case as the recognition of a constitutional 'right to hasten a person's inevitable death'[9]. The discussion is not without importance. If it were a constitutional right, after all, the freedom of states to regulate end-of-life decisions would be seriously limited. If not, it is really left to the 'laboratory of the states' – who have jurisdiction over this matter – to do so.

Whether a constitutional right or only a common law right, the courts always recognized that the right to refuse treatment is not absolute. Countervailing state interests can justify its restriction[10]. They include: preserving life, preventing suicide, maintaining the integrity of the medical profession and protecting innocent third parties. The state's interest in preserving life is the most common justification for intervention. It contains both a general notion of the sanctity of life and an interest in maintaining individual lives. When confronted with cases of treatment refusal, courts must carefully balance individual against state interests. The intrusiveness of any medical intervention and its prognosis are key factors in this balancing of interests. The right to refuse treatment becomes more forceful when the chances of recovery are diminishing and the degree of bodily invasion increases. On the basis of these criteria, courts have had few problems in recognizing that competent patients who are terminally ill have the right to refuse medical treatment. There is more uncertainty as to, on the one hand, the right of competent but **not** terminally ill patients and, on the other hand, incompetent patients.

Many of the cases of competent but not terminally-ill patients have to do with the refusal of blood transfusions by Jehovah's Witnesses. In one early case, a court made the interests of a 7-month-old child (in having a mother) prevail over those of its mother, a Jehovah's Witness who refused to receive blood[3]. Other state courts, however, respected refusals of blood transfusion, even when it involved parents with young children[3,4]. More recently, in 1993, a quadriplegic prisoner's right to refuse feeding and medical treatment was also recognized by the California Supreme Court, even though the patient was not terminally ill[11].

Incompetent patients' right to forego treatment can be exercised, on their behalf, by proxy decision makers or on the basis of living wills. In the Cruzan case, however, the US Supreme Court ruled that states may impose strict standards of proof for determining what incompetent patients would have wanted. Nancy Cruzan was lingering in a permanent vegetative state as the result of a car accident. Her parents requested to terminate her life support. Because Missouri, where Cruzan was hospitalized, requires 'clear and convincing evidence' of patients' preferences, this was rejected. The Supreme Court thus allowed states to employ a so called 'subjective test' for determining whether treatment of incompetent individuals may be foregone. According to this subjective test, decisions on behalf of incompetent patients must be based on previously expressed preferences. How clear the expression must be has been approached differently by various courts[3] and legislators. A written document is obviously strong evidence, but other factors are also taken into consideration by the courts. These include previous statements, the maturity of patients at the time statements were made, religious views, a pattern of treatment decisions and so on[3,4].

Very often, patients have not expressed their preferences clearly. Some state courts refuse to consider quality-of-life factors in deciding for incompetent patients. Others invoke their best interest and seek a balance between those and the state's interest in protecting life[3,4]. In this approach, which has been labelled as the 'objective test', treatment may be withheld or withdrawn if the burdens of treatment clearly outweigh the benefits of further life. The medical diagnosis and prognosis, the degree of physical pain and suffering and the intrusiveness of the treatment are key factors in assessing the best interests of patients. These criteria might seem problematic when applied in the case of patients in a persistent vegetative state, who are not in severe pain and, if fed and hydrated, are not close to death[12,13]. Nevertheless, many courts have decided that their life support and food may be withheld due to their poor quality of life and negative medical prognosis[3].

Legislative initiatives: advance-directive legislation   The last decades have seen an escalation of advance directive legislation. Legislative intervention became necessary because of reluctance by physicians to withhold or withdraw treatment. This was partly due to their fear of massive liability claims under American law, which induced them to seek court approval before respecting a family's wish to halt treatment. The emphasis on personal autonomy by the courts and the tendency to recreate the 'real' will of incompetent patients has contributed to the decay of traditional proxy decision making. Federal and state legislators have been forced to turn the wheel by explicitly regulating advance directives.

Under the Constitution, the federal government has in principle no jurisdiction over advance-directive legislation. Nevertheless, it has tried to interfere in this matter on the basis of its spending power. The federal Patient Self-Determination Act of 1991[14] aims at promoting the use of written instructions for future health-care preferences in order to facilitate treatment decisions for incompetent patients. It dictates that all health-care institutions receiving federal funding must inform patients about the advance-directive legislation of their state and the possibility of refusing treatment. Although it is doubtful that this Act will really stimulate patients to draft advance directives, providing the information might indeed be essential. Every state has its own advance directive legislation and large discrepancies exist from one to another[12,15]. Two types of directive have been introduced: living wills and proxy appointments (also called 'health care agent' or 'durable power of attorney'). The former regulate how written treatment preferences (living wills) are to be established and to what extent they are binding. The latter determine how surrogate decision makers are appointed, what their powers are and how they make treatment decisions. Although most states have statutes dealing with both living wills and the designation of a proxy, two states (Alabama and Alaska) explicitly authorize only the use of living wills and three (Massachusetts, Michigan and New York) have only proxy legislation[16]. Discrepancies between statutes involve both the formal requirements of advance directives and their substance. Several statutes permit only removal of 'life-sustaining procedures' for the 'terminally ill', for example, and others still differentiate artificial hydration and nutrition from other medical treatments, contrary to current doctrine and case law[3,12]. Most prohibit even withdrawal or withholding of treatment in case of pregnancy, although this might violate women's constitutional rights[12,15]. Advance directives help reduce conflicts among physicians, patients and families but cannot eradicate them, because most people do not have these directives[16,17]. Fortunately, 24 states have now enacted legislation stipulating that, in the absence of advance directives, family members, in some states even friends, may act as surrogate decision makers[12].

Active euthanasia and physician-assisted suicide: is there a constitutional right to assisted suicide?

Active euthanasia, the direct killing of another person, remains prohibited under the criminal law of all states. Whether done at the victim's request or not and whatever the motives, killing another person can lead to charges of murder, manslaughter or homicide[18]. Initiatives to legalize euthanasia in Washington (1991) and California (1992) were rejected in popular votes by 54% majorities[18,19].

Right-to-die organizations have chosen assisted suicide as the first station on the road to legalizing euthanasia. A legal battle is being fought on this issue, which is still a crime in most states. According to the Hemlock Society, 42 states prohibit assisted suicide, either under their statutory or common law, although the law is unclear in another 7 states[20]. The only state that introduced legislation permitting the practice is Oregon. During the 1994 federal elections, a measure legalizing physician-assisted suicide was approved by a 51 to 49% majority of the popular vote.[21] Measure 16 allowed a physician to prescribe lethal doses of medication to a competent, adult patient whose life expectancy is lower than 6 months. Procedural safeguards were built in to avoid abuses and ensure choice: a confirmation of the diagnosis by a second physician was necessary; the patient had to produce 1 written and 2 oral requests; the written request had to be signed by 2 witnesses; waiting periods of 15 days from the first oral request and 48 hours from the written request had to be respected; and the patient had to be referred for counselling to a specialist if depressed or suffering from a psychological disorder. The Oregon measure inspired others. In more than 10 states, legislation to allow assisted suicide has been introduced[22]. However, Oregon Measure 16 never entered into effect. On 3 August 1995, a federal District Judge struck it down as unconstitutional, after having issued a preliminary injunction some months earlier. Some terminally ill patients, with a history of depression, claimed that the measure violated the constitutional Equal Protection and Due Process clauses and the Americans with Disabilities Act and that it infringed on the Freedoms of Association and Exercise of Religion. Judge Hogan, who only dealt with the Equal Protection clause, ruled that the measure arbitrarily 'withholds from terminally ill citizens the same protections from suicide the majority enjoys'. He stressed that a treating physician was not qualified to evaluate potential mental impairments of suicide applicants. 'With state-sanctioned and physician assisted death at issue', the Judge warned, 'some 'good results' cannot outweigh other lives lost due to unconstitutional errors and abuses'[23].

But, court procedures have also been introduced in other states to challenge the constitutionality of prohibitions on assisted suicide. It is argued that these prohibitions violate the constitutionally protected liberty interest in controlling one's life. Michigan, where Dr Jack Kevorkian has already assisted at more than 20 suicides, has been at the forefront of this debate. In a 1992 attempt to stop Kevorkian, the Michigan legislature introduced a temporary ban on assisted suicide, later replaced by a permanent statute. Kevorkian and his supporters questioned the constitutionality of this ban. In December 1994, the Michigan Supreme Court ruled that there was no constitutional right to assisted suicide and that states had the authority to prohibit it[20]. Kevorkian's appeal to the federal Supreme Court was rejected in April 1995. A federal court in New York and the 9th Circuit Court (a federal appeal court) also ruled that there is no constitutional right to assisted suicide.

Rejecting the existence of a 'constitutional right to assisted suicide' seems wise. Indeed, if one combines the 'right to end one's life' with the notion of 'equal protection', it could become difficult to allow only physician-assisted suicide and limit it to cases of terminally ill but competent patients. If allowing patients to refuse life saving treatment while prohibiting the prescription of lethal doses to other patients amounts to unequal treatment, one is likely to say the same of the difference between prescribing lethal doses and killing paralysed patients who are unable to commit suicide[24]. It would then also be perceived as unfair to remove the 'right to die' simply because patients are incompetent and have not been able to express their preferences clearly. Constitutional arguments for or against euthanasia and physician-assisted suicide might simply not be the most appropriate ones. If the Supreme Court had recognized a constitutional right to suicide it would have opened the floodgates and fostered unlimited euthanasia.

Treatment refusal, assisted suicide and euthanasia under Canadian law

In relation to decisions near the end of life, Canadian law is more uniform than American. Criminal law, which prohibits active euthanasia and assisted suicide, is a federal matter and therefore uniform throughout

Canada. Moreover, few provinces have enacted advance-directive legislation. Therefore, general principles of common law determine what weight should be given to advance directives and substitute decisions in all common-law provinces. Common-law cases are often given authority even by Quebec civil law courts[25]. (Quebec is the only Canadian province with a civil law system, based on the, now reformed, Civil Code.)

Withholding and withdrawing of treatment

There are relatively few cases of treatment refusal in Canada. This seems to be the result of a consensus on the idea that treatment should be terminated if there is no sound medical reason to continue. There has been a discussion as to whether some provisions of the Criminal Code could create criminal liability on the part of physicians who withdraw or withhold treatment[25-27]. According to the Criminal Code, individuals are prohibited from endangering the lives of others by their acts or omissions and are obliged to provide 'the necessaries of life' to persons under their charge. The Criminal Code also decrees that physicians who undertake medical treatment that might endanger the lives of patients must use 'reasonable knowledge, skill and care in doing so'. In order to avoid misinterpretation of these provisions, the Law Reform Commission of Canada recommended that amendments to the Criminal Code be made.[28,29] Amendments were introduced in Parliament but were never adopted.[30] The Commission argued that the Criminal Code does not require physicians to provide medical treatments if these contradict the expressed wishes of patients, or if they are 'therapeutically useless' and not in their best interest. It is now generally accepted that the criminal law does not prohibit cessation of treatment. The 'reasonable physician' must respect standard medical practice and has no duty to prolong life at any price. On the contrary: aggressively delaying the inevitable, against the wishes or interest of the patient, is a violation of standard medical practice and could entail criminal liability for assault.[25,26]

In fact, the common-law doctrine of informed consent and the right to self-determination clearly prohibit physicians from performing medical treatments without consent. In *Malette vs Schulman*[31], the Ontario Court of Appeal ruled that a physician was liable in battery when he submitted a Jehovah's Witness to a blood transfusion after having read her written request not to receive blood. According to the court, the state has a strong interest in protecting life, but this interest does not override the common-law right to refuse treatment.

The right to refuse treatment is also clearly accepted under the civil law of Quebec. The Civil Code provides explicitly that no person may be submitted to medical care without her consent. The significance of this rule was clarified in *Nancy B. vs Hôtel-Dieu de Québec*[32] in which the court held that Nancy B.'s request to be disconnected from a respirator had to be respected. She had Guillain-Barré syndrome, a neurological disorder that left her irreversibly paralysed and dependent on a respirator. Her intellectual faculties, though, were not affected. In his decision, the judge stressed that this was not a case of homicide or suicide but merely cessation of treatment, which would allow her to die a natural death.

Indeed, the law treats treatment refusal and suicide differently. Physicians may discontinue treatment, but they may not assist in suicide. Nevertheless, Canadian courts recognize that this prohibition does not imply that one should always treat suicidal patients against their will. In *AG British Columbia vs Astaforoff*[31], the British Columbia Supreme Court held that the provincial prison authorities were not obliged to force-feed an inmate who was consciously starving herself to death. The court confirmed that every person has a duty to use reasonable care in preventing suicide but held that force-feeding was unreasonable. It stressed that the decision was made in light of the circumstances of the case: force-feeding of an unwilling person was not without danger; the woman was frail and the treatment intrusive; the procedure would have been necessary for a long time and she likely would do the same thing again. The circumstances were different in another case, in which a refugee swallowed a steel wire and refused food as a protest against his deportation. The Quebec Superior Court authorized forced treatment and feeding to save his life[34].

If patients are incompetent, decisions must be made by those who, in accordance with provincial laws, may represent them[35]. Some of the Canadian provinces explicitly recognize that competent individuals may appoint substitute decision makers to act on their behalf. In the absence of appointed proxies, provincial laws provide for a system of guardianship or tutorship. In most cases, close family members are appointed to represent incompetent patients. Proxies must act in the best interest of every patient. The Law Reform Commission pointed out that '[the incompetent patient's] 'best' interests do not **necessarily** involve the initiation or continuation of treatment' and that 'the law should recognize that the incapacity of a person to express his wishes is not sufficient a reason to oblige a physician to administer useless treatment for the purpose of prolonging his life'[29]. Physicians should be guided, in other words, by the dictates of sound medical practice.

When physicians or other health-care professionals are of the opinion that a proxy's treatment refusal is not in the best interest of an incompetent patient, they may request authorization from the court to provide treatment. This has been done frequently in cases where parents refused blood transfusions for their children. The Supreme Court recently made clear that although parents are best placed to nurture children and ensure their well-being, they do not have the right to refuse life saving blood transfusions. In *B. vs Children's Aid Society of Metropolitan Toronto*[36], the court rejected parents' argument that the liberty and freedom of religion clauses of the Canadian Charter of Rights gave the right, as Jehovah's Witnesses, to make the decision for their child. On the other hand, refusal of blood transfusion by mature minors has been accepted by courts in Canada.

Assisted suicide and active euthanasia

While there is a relative consensus on treatment refusal, euthanasia and assisted suicide have also been the subject of heated debate in Canada. Both are clearly prohibited under the Criminal Code. Attempted suicide has been decriminalized for some time now, but counselling, aiding or abetting a person to commit suicide can lead to imprisonment for up to 14 years. Killing another person is punishable as culpable homicide (murder or manslaughter). Feelings of compassion or even the victim's consent do not change the nature of the act. Some argue that the common-law defence of necessity or even a new 'defence of mercy' may be invoked either to justify the mercy killing of suffering patients or to lessen the sentence[29]. But, the intention of causing death is enough to categorize an act as murder. So, all cases of euthanasia, being the active killing for compassionate reasons, can be considered murder. S.235 of the Criminal Code prescribes 'imprisonment for life' as the minimum sentence for murder. The Law Reform Commission, which opposes the legalization of euthanasia or assisted suicide, recognized in its Working Paper that it could be reasonable to reduce the sentence for those acts motivated by mercy[29]. There was recently some debate on this issue after a Saskatchewan father was sentenced to life imprisonment for killing his 12-year-old daughter, bedridden with cerebral palsy. She required continuous care and was, according to the family, in terrible pain. Even though the decision was very severe for this caring father, organizations for the handicapped were understandably troubled by suggestions that this case proved the necessity of legalizing euthanasia. On 18 July 1995, the Saskatchewan Court of Appeal confirmed the judgment of the lower court. It stated that the minimum sentence for murder, as provided for by the Criminal Code, is not a 'cruel and unusual' punishment, prohibited by the Canadian Charter of Rights and Freedoms. Furthermore, the prohibition of euthanasia did not infringe the Charter right to 'life, liberty and security of the person'. The Court also dismissed the request for a 'constitutional exemption' based on these Charter provisions[37]. In the same period, a more compassionate judgment was obtained in front of an Ontario Court, which imposed a non-custodial sentence in a case of mercy-killing. In this case, an 80-year-old woman was charged with manslaughter, after killing her husband who suffered from Alzheimer's disease and consequential depression.

In Canada, the debate on assisted suicide has revolved around the case of Sue Rodriguez. She suffered from amyotrophic lateral sclerosis, a degenerative disease that inevitably leads to a total loss of physical control and results in dependence on a respirator and artificial feeding. As Rodriguez felt her strength diminishing, she launched a legal crusade to have her right to assisted suicide recognized by the courts. More than anything else, her battle was the expression of a desire to remain 'in control' over her life and body, a way of coping with the terrible disease that was slowly undermining her[1]. The Canadian Supreme Court rejected her bid with a 5 to 4 majority[38]. Though recognizing that the prohibition of assisted suicide deprived her of autonomy and impinged on the security of her person, the majority ruled that the restriction was justified on the basis of state interest in protecting the sanctity of life. They avoided the question of whether this prohibition discriminates against those who are unable to commit suicide without assistance. If the ruling had discriminatory effects, the Court argued, it could still have been justified under the Canadian Charter, because there was a pressing and substantial reason for it. As one observer remarked, both the majority and the minority failed to recognize that Rodriguez was not so much claiming a private right to kill herself, but 'the right to publicly ratify, in court, a new form of cooperative action bent upon inducing a certain person's death, at a certain time, and in a certain way'[39]. The question of whether there is really a 'right to suicide' was neglected by the judges. Indeed, the judges did not pay attention to the fact that decriminalizing suicide does not make suicide a fundamental right. Humanitarian reasons are at the origin of its decriminalization, and not a concern to establish some new right[6].

Although Rodriguez did not obtain legal approval by the highest court, her legal struggle and subsequent physician-assisted death provoked a debate that might lead eventually to a revision of Canada's assisted-suicide and euthanasia laws. Proposals were introduced in Parliament to grant immunity from prosecution to qualified physicians who assist competent patients in committing suicide. The federal Senate set up a 'Special Committee on Euthanasia and Assisted Suicide'. In its final report, a majority of the Committee recommended, among others, that both euthanasia and assisted suicide remain prohibited in all circumstances, but that the legislator provide for a less severe penalty in cases on mercy-killing[40]. A minority proposed to legalize assisted suicide and euthanasia in specific circumstances and sketched appropriate guidelines for such legalization. The Committee also reiterated that amendments to the Criminal Code should clarify the right to refuse treatment. It urged provincial and national governments to make palliative care a health care priority. Provinces and territories were advised to adopt advance directive legislation. The Committee thus suggested a sensible but cautious approach that characterizes Canadian law on these issues: federal and provincial governments should stimulate palliative care, should facilitate adequate relief of pain, and should assure that the public is informed about the right to refuse treatment; government should not, however, step onto the slippery slope of legalizing assisted suicide and euthanasia.

Conclusions

This overview indicates how the right to withhold or withdraw treatment is principally accepted under both American and Canadian law. Problems still arise when this right has to be exercised on behalf of incompetent patients. There is a tendency to recognize that, even in the case of incompetent patients, withholding or withdrawing treatment can be the most reasonable action. In the US, advance directives have been promoted to solve this problem. In both countries, the right to refuse treatment has lately been used for questioning the validity of laws prohibiting assisted suicide. Constitutional liberty and equality rights have been invoked to challenge criminal law provisions on assisted suicide. Most courts have rejected these arguments. One court ruled that, on the contrary, the Oregon legislation, allowing physicians to prescribe legal drugs to patients, deprives terminally ill patients of equal protection under the law. We are far from a legal recognition of a 'right to be killed' in Canada and the US, but further legal initiatives and intense political debate are to be expected.

Addendum March '96

Since the submission of this article, an important new decision on assisted suicide was rendered in the US, somehow at odds with the trend described earlier in this chapter. On March 6, 1996, in *Compassion in Dying* v. *Washington* (1996 WL 94848(9th Cir.(Wash.)), the 9th circuit court, rehearing the case *en banc*, overruled the decision of a three-judge panel of the same court mentioned earlier. The court ruled that there is a constitutional liberty interest in determining the time and manner of one's death, which can be limited by countervailing state interests. The Court concluded that the Washington statute, making it a felony to assist in suicide, violates the Constitution's Due Process Clause insofar as it prohibits physicians from prescribing life-ending medication for terminally ill, competent patients. It suggested that there is no relevant distinction between assisted suicide and the right to reject treatment or to receive pain-relieving drugs that hasten death. This decision could have serious consequences for the law on assisted suicide in the 9 states that fall under the jurisdiction of the 9th circuit (e.g. California and Oregon).

Acknowledgements

I am very grateful to Bartha Knoppers, Benjamin Freedman and Charles Weijer for continuous support and comments, and to Paul Nathanson for editorial work.

References

1   Lemmens T. Euthanasia and the good life. *Perspect Biol Med* 1995; **39**(1): 15–27

2   *In re* Conroy. *N.J.* 1985; **98**: 321; *A.2d* 1985; **486**: 1209

3   Eaton TE, Larson EJ. Experimenting with the 'Right to Die' in the Laboratory of the States. *Georgia Law Rev* 1991; **25**: 1253–326

4   Euthanasia, is it murder or mercy killing? A comparison of the criminal laws in the United States, The Netherlands and Switzerland. *Loyola of Los Angeles Int Comp Law J* 1990; **12**: 821–43

5   Cruzan vs Director, Missouri Department of Health. *U.S.* 1990; **261**: 280

6   Kamisar Y. Are laws against assisted suicide unconstitutional? *Hastings Cent Rep* 1993; **23**(3): 32–41

7   Kass LR. Is there a right to die? *Hastings Cent Rep* 1993; **23**(1): 34–46

8   Robertson J. Cruzan and the constitutional status of nontreatment decisions for incompetent patients. *Georgia Law Rev* 1991; **25**: 1139–202

9   Sedler RA. The constitution and hastening inevitable death. *Hastings Cent Rep* 1993; **23**(5): 20–5

10 DiCamillo JA. A comparative analysis of the right to die in The Netherlands and the United States after Cruzan: reassessing the right of self-determination. *Am Univ J Int Law Policy* 1992; 7: 807–42

11 Thor vs Superior Court. *P.2d* 1993; **855**: 375; discussed in JMW. Court affirms prisoner's right to refuse life-sustaining treatment. *J Law, Med Ethics* 1994; **22**: 92

12 Tarantino LM. Withdrawal of life support: conflict among patient wishes, family, physicians, courts and statutes, and the law. *Buffalo Law Rev* 1994; **42**: 623–52

13 Dresser RS. Autonomy revisited: the limits of anticipatory choices. In: Binstock RH, Post SG, Whitehouse PJ. eds. *Dementia and aging; ethics, values, and policy choices*. Baltimore: Johns Hopkins University, 1992: 71–85

14 Giving life to patient self-determination. *Hastings Cent Rep* 1993; **23**(1): 12–24

15 Gelfand G. Living will statutes: the first decade. *Wisconsin Law Rev* 1987; 737–822

16 Advance care planning. Priorities for ethical and empirical research. *Hastings Cent Rep Special Suppl* 1994; **24**(6): S1–S36

17 Areen J. Advance directives under state law and judicial decisions. *Law Med Health Care* 1991; **19**: 91–100

18 CeloCruz MT. Aid-in-dying: should we decriminalize physician-committed euthanasia? *Am J Law Med* 1992; **18**(4): 369–94

19 Capron AM. Even in defeat, proposition 161 sounds a warning. *Hastings Cent Rep* 1993; **23**(1): 32-33

20 Oregon's assisted suicide law stokes the fires of controversy. *State Health Notes* 20 February 1995; **16**(198): 1–3

21 Capron AM. Sledding in Oregon. *Hastings Cent Rep* 1995; **25**(1): 34–5

22 Legislators tackle physician aid-in-dying. *Hemlock TimeLines* 1995; **61**: 1–5

23 Lee vs Oregon [Civ. No. 94-6467-HO] 1995 WL 471792; 471797 (D.Or.)

24 Capron AM. Easing the passing. *Hastings Cent Rep* 1994; **24**(4): 25–6

25 Dickens BM. Medically assisted death: Nancy B. vs Hôtel-Dieu de Québec. *McGill Law J* 1993; **38**: 1053–70

26 Sneiderman B. The case of Nancy B.: a criminal law and social policy perspective. *Health Law J* 1993; **1**: 25–38

27 Downie J. Voluntary euthanasia in Canada. *Health law in Canada* 1993; **14**(1): 13–30

28 Law Reform Commission of Canada. *Report: euthanasia, aiding suicide and cessation of treatment.* Ottawa: Minister of Supply and Services, 1983

29 Law Reform Commission of Canada. *Working Paper 28: euthanasia, aiding suicide and cessation of treatment.* Ottawa: Minister of Supply and Services, 1982

30 Fish A, Singer PA. Nancy B.: the Criminal Code and decisions to forgo life-sustaining treatment. *CMAJ* 1992; **147**(5): 637–42

31 Malette vs Schulman. *Ontario Rep (2d)* 1990; **72**: 417

32 Nancy B. vs Hôtel-Dieu de Québec. *Dominium Law Rep (4th)* 1992; **86**: 385

33 British Columbia (AG) vs Astaforoff. *British Columbia Law Rep* 1983; **47**: 217

34 Canada (PG) vs Hôpital Notre Dame (Niemic third party). *Receuils de Jurisprudence du Québec* 1984; 426

35 Glass KC. *Elderly persons and decision-making in a medical context: challenging Canadian Law.* Doctoral Thesis McGill University, Montréal 1992

36 B. vs Children's Aid Society of Metropolitan Toronto, 27 January 1995, Supreme Court n.23298, unpublished

37 R. vs Latimer. (unreported judgement) Saskatchewan Court of Appeal [1995] S.J. No. 402

38 Rodriguez vs British Columbia (AG). *Dominium Law Rep (4th)* 1993; **107**: 342

39 Freedman B. The Rodriguez case: sticky questions and slippery answers. *McGill Law J* 1994; **39**: 644–56

40 *Report of the Special Senate Committee on euthanasia and assisted suicide: of life and death.* Ottawa: Minister of Supply and Services, 1995

Killing and letting die: a defensible distinction

Will Cartwright

Department of Philosophy, University of Essex, Colchester and Centre of Medical Law and Ethics, King's College, University of London, London, UK

The distinction between killing and letting die is investigated and clarified. It is then argued that in most cases, though not in all, it is worse to kill than to let die. In euthanasia the significance of the distinction is diminished, but still important.

There is a widely shared view that active and passive euthanasia are importantly different. It is said to be one thing (passive euthanasia) to let patients die, which may sometimes be permissible, but it is quite another (active euthanasia) to kill them, which never is. This discrimination between two forms of euthanasia has been forcefully attacked by certain philosophers on the ground that the underlying distinction between killing and letting die is either not clear or, if clear, not morally important. I propose to explore the nature of the distinction, its moral significance and its relevance to euthanasia.

The nature of the distinction

It is sometimes supposed that the distinction between killing and letting die exemplifies a more general and fundamental distinction between action and inaction, or action and omission, where action involves bodily movement and inaction or omission its absence. Thus, on this view, killing is moving one's body such that someone dies and letting die is failing to move it with the same result. But this is a mistake. Suppose that you are half way down a cliff face dangling from a rope and I am endeavouring to haul you to safety. Feeling myself being dragged over the cliff, I take my hands from the rope to save myself with the result that you die. Though I have acted by moving my hands, I have surely let you die rather than killed you.

A more plausible account of killing and letting die would be that one kills someone if one initiates a causal sequence that ends in his death, whereas one lets him die if one allows an already existing causal sequence to culminate in his death, when one could have prevented this upshot. This makes the distinction turn on how one stands to causal sequences that culminate in death rather than on whether one acts or not. Both

Postal address:
W Cartwright
Department of Philosophy,
University of Essex,
Wivenhoe Park,
Colchester
CO4 3SQ, Essex, UK

elements of the account need enriching. One can kill someone by sustaining an already existing causal sequence culminating in his death as well as by initiating such a sequence. Equally one can let someone die, not merely by failing to intervene in an existing lethal causal sequence, but also by removing an obstacle that is holding back such a sequence. This is what I did when I removed my hands from the rope from which you were dangling. My aid to you in hanging on to the rope held back the lethal sequence and in withdrawing that aid I removed the obstacle to the progress of the sequence[1].

But this account faces a difficulty for there seem to be cases of unblocking lethal sequences which are intuitively killing. Suppose that a fault in a nuclear power plant leads to heavy and potentially lethal emissions. A new protective shield is installed to halt the emissions. Someone subsequently removes it with the result that people die. This person has surely killed the victims rather than let them die, though the account above would seem to suggest otherwise. A way of dealing with this objection would be to say that, when the shield was installed, the original causal sequence was not so much blocked as eliminated. Thus when the culprit removed the shield, this amounted to, or at any rate more closely resembled, initiating a fresh causal sequence rather than releasing an existing one, and thus on the above account would rank as killing[2].

The moral significance of the distinction

Armed with this account of the distinction, let us turn to its moral significance. Using an imaginary example that has become famous, James Rachels has sought to deny that significance. Smith drowns his 6-year-old cousin in the bath by holding him under the water in order to inherit his fortune. Jones lets his 6-year-old cousin drown in the bath after he has slipped and hit his head, also to inherit his fortune. The cases are identical in terms of upshot and motive and the only difference seems to be that Smith killed his cousin whereas Jones let him die. Rachels asserts that there is no moral difference between the two cases, Jones's behaviour being as morally reprehensible as Smith's. He concludes that the distinction between killing and letting die is of no moral significance, and attributes our disposition to think otherwise to the influence of other features that are only contingently connected with the distinction. Thus those who let others die usually have less bad motives than those who kill, and the costs of saving people are usually higher than those incurred in not killing them. But when these motives and costs are equalised as in the example, the moral insignificance of the distinction is exposed[3].

Rachels's case involves two people in identical circumstances, one of whom kills and the other lets die. But if we now consider a different sort of case involving only one person who has to choose between killing and letting die, the distinction seems to resume its intuitive force. If the only way a doctor can save two people dying of organ failure is by killing a third person to obtain his organs for transplantation into them, we would surely regard such a killing as morally outrageous and the letting die, if it counts as that, as merely deeply regrettable. But Michael Tooley has produced an example of this sort where once again the distinction seems without force. You are to imagine a machine containing two children, John and Mary. If you push a button, John will die but Mary will emerge unscathed. If you do not push the button, Mary will die and John will emerge unscathed. If you push the button, you kill John; if you do not, you let Mary die. You are to assume that there is no reason to prefer one child to the other. Tooley thinks it a matter of moral indifference whether you push the button and kill or do not push it and let die, and recommends flipping a coin[4].

Tooley's moral judgement is open to question. As things stand, Mary is going to die. You can intervene by pressing the button and substitute John's death for Mary's, but it is not at all clear that you are morally entitled to do this in the absence of any good reason. By what right do you change who lives and who dies? But let us waive this point and accept for the sake of argument that in this case, and indeed in Rachels's, there is no moral difference between the killing and the letting die. What follows from this? One might presume that all that follows is that the distinction is not always morally significant. In fact Rachels and Tooley infer the much more powerful conclusion that it is not ever morally significant. They reason that if the distinction ever has moral force, that force must be present wherever the distinction is to be found. But since there are situations involving the distinction where it allegedly has no force, such as the examples given, then it follows that it never has such force.

This is a crucial mistake. The moral insignificance of the distinction in some cases does not entail its insignificance in all. However some explanation is called for as to how the distinction can matter in some cases and not in others. Two points can be made[5].

First killing and letting die should not be thought of as sharply differentiated homogeneous categories, but as heterogeneous groupings containing a variety of types, such that some of the types in one category are close to types in the other. Thus we have seen that killing covers not just initiating a lethal causal sequence, but also sustaining one and, as we shall shortly see, diverting one. It also covers, as seen earlier, some cases of removing an obstacle to a lethal sequence. On the other hand, letting die covers not just failing to intervene in an existing lethal sequence, but also unblocking a temporarily halted one. No doubt further types are encompassed by both categories, but we can already see that one type occurs in both, namely unblocking a causal sequence. Sometimes this will be an instance of killing, sometimes of letting die. Thus if we are comparing two cases of this type, one of which just falls in the killing category and the other just in the letting die category, we would expect there to be little moral difference between them, whereas if we are comparing examples of the two categories that are further removed from each other, we would anticipate greater moral difference between them.

The second reason why the distinction between killing and letting die may have force in some cases but not in others, is that there are many factors that contribute to the determination of the rightness or wrongness of an act other than this one. These factors may interact in complex ways with each other. The moral force of the distinction between killing and letting die may be outweighed by other factors, or significantly altered or even rendered entirely nugatory by them.

These two reasons may be invoked to explain why the distinction seems to have no moral force in the Rachels and Tooley examples. The first reason does not seem to apply in the Rachels case because we have here straightforward cases of killing and letting die, one initiating a sequence and the other allowing a sequence to continue, that do not seem close to each other in the way explained. However the second reason does seem applicable. Both the killing and the letting die in this case are characterised by such an equally dreadful upshot, motive and stoniness of heart that the remaining difference between them, the killing and letting die, may be thought to be simply swamped and rendered inoperative as a morally compelling factor.

In the Tooley case the first reason specified above does seem to apply. If you push the button you kill John, but you do so, not by initiating a causal sequence, but by redirecting an existing one. For there was a lethal sequence already under way in the machine that would cause Mary's death unless stopped. Now redirecting a causal sequence does not involve initiating it, but nor does it just involve letting it continue. It lies in the space between the two. To the extent that the causal sequence already exists and is not stopped, it has something of allowing about it. To the extent that the sequence is redirected it resembles initiating to some degree. Thus though pressing the button is a case of killing, it is a case that has some resemblance to letting die, which would help to explain why, on one view of this case, there seems to be no moral difference between killing by pressing the button and letting die by not pressing it. Moreover, the second reason applies to this case as well. Whether or not the button is pressed, the outcome is identically bad, the life of an innocent child is senselessly terminated. Beside this predominant fact, the issue of whether the death occurs through a killing (particularly of this sort) or a letting die may pale into insignificance, rendered inconsequential by the larger factor. Thus these considerations enable us to see how the fact, if it is a fact, that the distinction between killing and letting die has no moral force in the Rachels and Tooley cases is compatible with its retaining that force in other cases.

But an adequate defence of the distinction requires more than limiting the effect of certain counter-examples to it. How much weight is carried by the fact, if it is one, that the distinction can explain our intuitions in a variety of cases is a matter of controversy. But whatever the answer to this, there remains the question of why the distinction matters. It is not presumably just an ultimate moral fact that killing is usually worse than letting die, but rather one that ought to admit of a deeper explanation. What explanations are available?

One emerges if we recall how the distinction was drawn above. In the paradigm cases, killing someone involves initiating a fatal causal sequence, whereas letting someone die involves allowing an existing fatal causal sequence to run its course. In the first case the cause of death is the person who initiated the fatal sequence, in the second it is the fatal sequence itself rather than the person who allowed it to continue. We attach moral importance to the form and degree of people's causal involvement in the deaths of others, and it is distinctions of causal involvement that explain the moral importance of the distinction between killing and letting die. Developing this explanation of the distinction further would require an investigation into the nature of causation, which is a controversial issue. On some accounts of causation a failure to prevent a death can count as the cause of it, but it seems to me plausible to suppose that an adequate account of causality is going to register significant causal distinctions of some form between killing and letting die.

A further explanation of the distinction's moral significance is to see it as reflecting a fundamental difference between two types of moral duty. We have duties not to harm others, which require restraint from us and may, therefore, be designated as negative duties. We have duties to help others, which require intervention from us and may, therefore, be designated as positive duties. These duties differ in both scope and force. Each of us is unable to render assistance to all who need it and so our positive duties are selective and circumscribed, whereas each of us is capable of avoiding harm to all others and so our negative duties are owed to all.

Furthermore, when positive and negative duties clash, when we can only help some by harming others, the negative duties are thought to take precedence. We conventionally suppose that we may not sacrifice some in order to render aid to others (e.g. transplants). To hold otherwise would be to fail to treat people with the respect that we think they deserve. Thus to breach a negative duty is standardly worse than to breach a positive duty. On this view then the reason why killing is generally morally worse than letting die is because the former is a breach of a negative duty and the latter is a breach of only a positive duty, if it is a breach of duty at all. This explanation could also be cast in terms of the negative and positive rights of potential victims[6].

The distinction and euthanasia

Applying the distinction to euthanasia raises further questions about both its nature and its moral force in this context.

Passive euthanasia involves not just letting the patient die, but doing so quite deliberately and for the good of the patient. In a similar way, active euthanasia is deliberately killing the patient for his own good. This means that withholding from a terminally ill patient treatment, which would extend his life a little but which is judged to be excessively burdensome, is not passive euthanasia. Withholding the treatment is to let the patient die and it is withheld for his own good, but the aim is not to end his life so much as to ensure his comfort in his remaining days. If, however, this is regarded as passive euthanasia, as it is by some, and it is then added that active euthanasia is morally indistinguishable from passive euthanasia, then those who accept such withholding of treatment, as most of us probably would, will be said to have no reason to flinch from active euthanasia. Endorsement of the former implies endorsement of the latter[7]. But both distinctions here demolished are worth preserving. Passive euthanasia needs to be distinguished both from active euthanasia and from withholding burdensome treatment. The subject of this essay has been the first distinction, and I can do no more here than assert the importance of the second, and add that the defence of it will hinge on difficult issues to do with intention. To suppose that withholding burdensome treatment from a patient is morally no different from active euthanasia seems to me to reveal a profligate disregard of distinctions which is calculated to have a morally flattening and coarsening effect.

Even when these distinctions have been clarified, we are still going to confront ambiguous cases. Consider the difficult and much discussed case of turning off a life support machine. This strikes some as letting die, others as killing. The latter view is typically inspired by the fact that action is required, the body has to be moved, to turn off the machine. But, as we have already seen, letting die can involve action too. Thus when I removed my hands from the rope and you fell to your death, I let you die despite the fact that I moved my hands. And turning off the life support machine may seem to be similar. In both cases a lethal sequence is temporarily blocked and the obstacle to its progress is then removed.

On the other hand we have met an apparently similar case which was one of killing. When the dangerous emissions from a nuclear power plant were blocked by a new shield, the subsequent removal of it and consequent deaths seemed evidently to be a case of killing and not letting die. The difference between this and the rope case is perhaps that in this case there is reason to say that the threat is eliminated rather than halted, and that the removal of the shield is the initiation of a new threat, whereas in the rope case the threat is not eliminated, but only restrained with considerable effort. Which of these two cases does turning off the mechanical life support more closely resemble? The answer is that it hovers uneasily between the two, in so far as the mechanical life support is an obstacle to the lethal sequence that is more stable and self-sustaining than the hands around the rope, but is less so than the shield in the nuclear plant[8].

Finally, does the distinction between active and passive euthanasia have moral force? I have argued that *prima facie* it does, in so far as it rests upon the distinction between killing and letting die, but I think that a number of considerations converge to make that force less than one would anticipate. First, the moral force of the distinction between killing and letting die partially flows from the distinction between negative and positive duties. Since duties not to injure carry more weight than duties to aid, infringements of the former, like killing, are more grave than infringements of the latter, like letting die. But some people, doctors amongst them, have particularly onerous positive duties to aid some others, such that the breach of those duties is scarcely less serious than the breach of their negative duties. This equalisation of his duties means that for a doctor deliberately to let his patient die may not seem notably less bad than killing him. Secondly, in the case where the patient requests euthanasia, where the moral case for it is strongest, the effect of that request, according to those who favour euthanasia, is to release the doctor from his negative and positive duties towards the patient, with respect to killing and letting die. Since it is the differential force of those duties that partly engenders the moral discrepancy between killing and letting die, the cancellation of those duties presumably also cancels the moral discrepancy in question, leaving it *pro tanto* a matter of moral indifference in these circumstances whether the euthanasia is active or passive. Thirdly, I have argued that, while the distinction between killing and letting die has moral force, that force may be weakened or even annulled when this distinction interacts in complex ways with other morally relevant factors. In most situations in which people are killed or allowed to die, the death is a bad thing. This is a pervasive feature of those contexts in which our judgments about the respective merits of killing and letting die are formed. But in the context of euthanasia this feature is reversed: the death is now deemed to be a good thing. This reversal may have an effect on the moral force of the distinction between killing and letting die, weakening or even cancelling it. Perhaps when death is a good thing for the patient, it really does not matter any longer whether it is accomplished actively or passively.

There is, however, a consideration which pulls in the other direction. I suggested above that the moral distinction between killing and letting die rested not merely on the asymmetry of negative and positive duties, but also on a causal asymmetry. The cause of death in a case of killing is the agent who initiates the causal sequence; in a case of letting die it is the lethal causal sequence. Even if in a case of voluntary euthanasia conducted by a doctor the asymmetry of positive and negative duties is no longer at work, and even if the fact that it is for the patient's own good affects the moral force of the distinction between killing and letting die, the causal asymmetry between the two remains and invests the distinction with a residual moral importance. We regard life as having an intrinsic value as well as a value to the person whose life it is. When it has ceased to be of value to that person, we therefore still regard its destruction as a matter of the utmost moral gravity. Even if we persuade ourselves that its destruction is the right thing in the circumstances, it seems morally preferable, other things being equal, to accomplish that end by means that render our causal involvement limited and indirect rather than central and direct. Thus we pay our respects to the value extinguished.

References

1 Foot P. The problem of abortion and the doctrine of the double effect. In: Foot P. *Virtues and vices*. Oxford: Blackwell, 1978: 19–32
2 McMahan J. Killing, letting die, and withdrawing aid. *Ethics* 1993; **103**: 250–79
3 Rachels J. Active and passive euthanasia. *N Engl J Med* 1975; **292**: 78–80
4 Tooley M. An irrelevant consideration: killing versus letting die. In: Steinbock B, Norcross A. eds. *Killing and letting die*. 2nd edn. New York: Fordham University, 1994: 103–11
5 McMahan J. *op.cit.* 272–7
6 Foot P. *op.cit.*
7 Rachels J. *op.cit.*
8 McMahan J. *op.cit.* 265–8

Theological perspectives

Rowan Williams

Bishopstow, Newport, Gwent, UK

Most discussions of Christian attitudes to euthanasia presuppose that the grounds for a Christian critique of the practice are: (i) a commitment to the 'sanctity of human life'; and (ii) the prohibition against killing the innocent, i.e. breaking the norm of not taking human life in anything other than circumstances where another person directly and deliberately threatens one's own life or that of others. The fact that Christians, at least since the time of St Augustine, have condemned suicide reinforces the idea that the first principle mentioned rules out any decision by persons suffering even the most acute mental or physical pain to terminate their life. Augustine's discussion in the nineteenth book of *The City of God*[1] takes place in the context of a polemic against what he believes to be the Stoic position that, in certain circumstances, suicide is commendable: the Stoics, he says, hold that material life is the supreme good for human beings, and that appropriate states of mind (detachment and self-control) can guarantee the continuation of a sense of well-being in more or less any adversity; but at the same time they recognise that some evils may be so severe that the best and most rational course of action is to end one's life. Augustine underlines the inconsistency in this and, in contrast, offers a picture in which life is naturally vulnerable and uncertain, incapable of being securely protected against pain, whether by inner detachment or outer prosperity: if we can properly learn that our mortal life is inherently liable to suffering, we can learn patience and fortitude, and, most importantly of all, hope – the confidence that true and lasting happiness is to be found elsewhere than in this world. He has already argued, in the first book of the same work[2], that suicide is a subdivision of homicide, and that no suicide can be a case of *magnitudo animi*, generosity of soul; and here, in the nineteenth book, he elaborates his case against the widespread opinion among cultivated Romans that suicide in the face of acute suffering or public humiliation is not only acceptable but courageous and admirable.

Underlying his polemic is not only the biblical prohibition against homicide, but also the conviction that self-preservation is a fundamental natural 'given' in human beings. If this principle is weakened, many other aspects of Augustine's analysis of Christian life and Christian virtue are put at risk. At the very least, the Christian must live 'rationally', that is in accordance with the place human beings are meant to occupy in creation overall. Suicide represents, in this perspective, the attempt to step out

Postal address:
The Rt Revd The Lord
Bishop of Monmouth
Bishopstow, Newport,
Gwent NP9 4EA, UK

British Medical Bulletin 1996;**52** (No. 2):362–368

from an ordained position in the structure of things, to take charge of one's fate, in a way that cannot be 'rational'. Furthermore, Augustine always treats the love of self and the instinct of self-preservation as the fundamental case of love: if we do not love ourselves, if we do not happily consent to being the sort of beings we are and nurture the life that is ours, we shall not know how to love other realities for what they are and to nurture them in the way that best accords with the overall character of the universe. Love, at every point, requires just and true perception. If we step outside the bounds of God's created order, we lose the capacity to judge according to such perception; we distort our own vision and end up enslaving others to our preferences and whims. Augustine would doubtless have argued, in the contemporary debate, that anyone who believes it right or justifiable to take his or her own life in circumstances of pain or degradation would be only a short step away from wanting to take such a decision on behalf of another. If I do not correctly prize my life, I shall not correctly prize the lives of others.

This remains the majority position of Christians of all traditions. It is given further reinforcement by some aspects of Reformation theology, particularly the strong emphasis in classical Lutheranism on divine vocation: all persons have a calling from God unique to themselves, realisable at any and every moment of their lives; so that the taking of one's own life is seen as a refusal of this calling. The same thing appears more obliquely in the context of counter-Reformation (Catholic) spirituality, where some writers encourage deliberate meditation on possible future disasters or evils, so as to practise resignation in advance. The Anglo-Welsh monk, Augustine Baker (1575–1641), composed a series of 'Particular Acts of Resignation', including resigning oneself to 'pains, deformity, horror in the sight of others . . . disfiguring in my face, or distortions in other parts of my body. . . . That my body should by little and little putrefy and rot away, . . . To die without senses or memory, and distracted or mad' – and so forth, for several pages[4]. In such a frame of reference, a decision to end one's life becomes a statement that **this** particular state of existence is not capable of being lived through to God's glory. It is the precise opposite of the mentality of the 'living will': both, it might be said, are efforts to pre-empt the results of being in a condition where we are incapable of rational reflection; but the one attempts to guarantee that no internal or external condition be allowed to qualify the willingness to be obedient to God in every scene of life, while the other attempts to guarantee that no circumstance should rob me of my freedom to assess my condition and respond to it appropriately and reasonably – it being taken for granted that one such reasonable response would be to end my life.

It should perhaps be added at this stage that the impression of *passivity* in the face of acute suffering that might be given by some of the material mentioned is not the whole picture. It is obviously taken for granted by a writer like Augustine that the active alleviation of suffering is part of the 'justice' that is also a fundamental aspect of this world-view, a justice that consists in wishing for every other subject the same level of good one wishes for oneself, and acting accordingly. And, for both the earlier and the later discussion of 'resignation' to the evils of the world, it is axiomatic that there are circumstances where the option of simply alleviating pain is not possible. It is also worth noting that no Christian theologian ever asserts that the preservation of human life *at all costs* is an ethical imperative. This would make nonsense of any kind of risk for the sake of a greater good, of martyrdom, ultimately of the crucifixion of Jesus Christ. Accordingly, modern discussion has generally seen the withdrawal of life-support systems as quite compatible, in some conditions, with the general moral principles enunciated above[5]. For a strict Christian moralist, euthanasia would not (contrary to what some Christians and non-Christians seem to think) consist in **any** medical or therapeutic measure that resulted in the death of a patient, but only in the deliberate *initiating* of a process whose *primary* intent and effect would be to cause a patient's death. Some theologians have pointed out the ironies of the current situation in which pressure for freedom to terminate life can coexist with the assumption that the prolongation of physical life is a major imperative for the physician, and that anything else represents a kind of defeat for the resources of medical skill.

However, it has to be admitted that the theological tradition I have been describing has some highly problematic elements. Augustine relies heavily on the idea that this present existence is an opportunity for learning those virtues that will secure our bliss in the world to come; and there is no doubt that this can produce (and has produced) a style of moralising about suffering that is itself morally problematic. The idea that acute mental or physical distress is presented to us as an occasion for self-improvement overlooks the manifest fact that such distress itself affects our emotions and judgements, our abilities to respond to situations. Suffering not only weakens, it sometimes 'corrupts' – that is, it erodes our moral creativity or engenders resentment and bitterness. And this is not simply the result of a refusal to rise to the challenge: it is part of the suffering itself. More has to be said here, if we are not to appear to be simply recommending a rather vacuous heroism. It is also true that Augustine's assumptions about the rational ordering of the universe as a ground for ethical decisions are by no means so clear as earlier generations might have thought. Augustine takes for granted a world in which the natures of created things stand in fixed and hierarchical relation to each other, so that their places in the overall scheme prescribe what attitudes are to be adopted towards them and what is legitimate for them. But this depended, in Augustine's day, on treating certain definitions of how things fitted into the patterns of being as self-evident – the soul is 'higher' than the body, for example, and man is more inherently spiritual than woman. The world most moderns take for granted (rightly or wrongly) does not contain so many apparently fixed points, and we are far more suspicious of injunctions resting on patterns claimed to be self-evident. And finally although the intention of much of this language is not to commend passivity, its practical **effect** has often been just this. Baker's acts of resignation seem to leave the onus of proof rather on anyone who claims that fates such as those imagined in his meditations could rightly and reasonably be avoided. Baker is **not** a fatalist, any more than Augustine is; but a presumption of fatalism can easily creep in, especially if any possible suffering or humiliation is seen as an opportunity for spiritual growth.

That being said, I believe that there are several aspects of this tradition that continue to be of pertinence for discussion of the acceptability of euthanasia (defined in the way I suggested earlier). First of all, from the point of view of the sufferer who might be tempted to consider the various options associated with a 'living will', i.e. a declaration of preferences for actions to be taken in the event of terminal and incapacitating conditions: Augustine's argument suggests that how I regard my own condition is not exclusively **my** business; it is inextricably bound up with how I relate to others, and it communicates a general perspective. If I mortgage my options in advance as regards how I am going to react to certain outcomes, if I declare my unwillingness to continue to bear this or that particular level of suffering, am I implicitly declaring that a life lived in that condition is not worth living? And if so, what message does that send, not only to some other person struggling to continue under comparable conditions, but to physicians making decisions on comparable cases? Is my decision another piece of evidence that condition X is intolerable, so that there will be a presumption that lives lived with condition X are 'natural' candidates for termination? In short, it may be that an advance declaration that I am not willing to go on living beyond a certain level of physical or mental deterioration and that I should wish active measures to be taken to bring death closer could have the effect of altering the 'currency value' of perceptions of the condition I regard as intolerable and increasing the presumption that termination is a, or the, proper response. Equally, however, a decision to refuse certain kinds of palliative treatment or technological intervention can also send out a significant message – that physical survival is not the sole moral good in such circumstances, and that discerning when to let go, not of life as such but of the will to stay alive at all costs, is a moral skill worth cultivating. Thus, the expressed desire not to avail oneself of all available resources to prolong life, while declining to specify any circumstances in which I or anyone else would be justified in intervening to end it, is a coherent Christian position, which honours the main elements of the tradition. As one or two medical ethicists in the US have put it, the right to refuse treatment is a more promising subject for exploring the complexities of this whole area than the supposed 'right to die'. In Stanley Hauerwas's words, the sometimes awkward distinctions drawn between 'ordinary' and 'extraordinary' means of prolonging life resulted from the desire of Christians 'to balance their sense that their lives were not at their disposal with their sense that death is not to be opposed unconditionally'[6]. This, I believe, is a helpful formulation for the course the theological moralist has to steer.

Behind such a position lies a version of that doctrine of Christian vocation to which I made reference earlier. At every moment of our biological life, we are summoned and enabled to form a response to God that expresses back to God something of God's own life and glory. Our biological life is, for the Christian, a gift from God, an expression of the divine generosity, but it is not a *thing* we possess, to hold or relinquish in any straightforward sense. God makes us with the potential to reflect back to him what he is, and the gift of life is simply the condition of our thus fulfilling our potential. This is one way of spelling out the meaning of the belief that we are made in God's image. Now to maintain life in adversity and to communicate something of God's self-consistency in so doing is one kind of calling; to *risk* the life we are given for God's sake is another; to refuse to cling to or protect that life is another – even in circumstances where we are morally and practically sure that death will eventuate. But to decide to end a life is to put oneself outside the whole frame of reference – to cease to play this game or speak this language. Whatever its rationale, it cannot be a specifically Christian one, and the Christian tradition gives us no way of theologising about it. It echoes the famous metaphor of Ivan Karamazov in Dostoyevsky's novel *The Brothers Karamazov* about 'returning our tickets'[7]. The risking of life in the more or less certain knowledge of impending death, the refusal of self-protection – these, like the patient endurance of pain, can show an aspect of the divine life, that aspect which for Christians is manifested in the incarnation, in which God the Word becomes the agent of a human life and, as such, exposed to the risks of mortality. But it is hard to see how the resignation of life because of its intolerable burden can express the nature and activity of God.

One further consideration may here be mentioned, a consideration to which, once again, recent American writing has drawn attention[8]. My life, my identity, exists not simply 'in' myself as an individual, but in the perceptions of myself that others have and the ways in which I enter into their construction of their lives, become part of them. Thus, a decision to end my life is inevitably a decision about the lives of others, about what will be offered or available to them. What is more, I have (in ways that can be disturbing) no control over how I enter the lives and self-constructions of others, nor any clear grasp of just how many other lives I am (in this sense) 'present' in, and how deeply or significantly I may be present. This poses a problem that is both moral and practical. In the first place, my lack of control over my presence in the lives of others puts in question any notion that I have a proprietary right over my continued existence such that I can 'withdraw' from these relationships, whose nature and significance I do not and cannot fully grasp. In the second place, if we were ever in the position of contemplating the licensing of euthanasia on the basis of consent by family, for example, rather than consent by the sufferer, we should be faced with the question of whose perceptions or reactions would be decisive or most properly relevant, and the subsidiary question of how conflicts might be resolved in such a situation. This is not, as such, a strictly theological observation, though it takes for granted a theological view (of the constitutive character of relations, chosen and unchosen, in determining our identity); but it might well be regarded as a factor influencing the way Christians would be likely to make up their minds on the morality of euthanasia.

The foregoing observations have deliberately not engaged with the specific complexities of legal or clinical policy. Their aim has been only to outline some of what has formed the traditional Christian response to the claim that euthanasia is a defensible moral option. I have concentrated on euthanasia as an option requested by the sufferer, as there would be few if any Christians who would seriously entertain the legitimacy of involuntary euthanasia, at the decision of clinicians or others. However, I have also tried to underline the fact that the traditional perspective, which remains that of (probably) the majority of Christians today, has no commitment to the idea that the preservation of life is in all circumstances the overriding imperative in clinical care. For this reason, I should be happy to see the phrase, 'the sanctity of life', disappear from the discussion, as it can easily give a false impression of past and present ethical theories informed by Christian theology. It is, in any case, a form of words unfamiliar in this context prior to the present century[9]. My emphasis has been rather on the theological doctrine of the divine image in human agents: this has (at least) a two-fold importance in the present debate: it stresses the human vocation to react creatively in all imaginable conditions (which may include the possibility of deciding not to seek artificial prolongation of life), to mirror the qualities of the divine action; and it reminds us of the complex interrelations binding our identities together in the human world, reflecting the relations that constitute the divine life as understood in the Christian doctrine of the Trinity. But perhaps the most searching point to emerge from a study of the Christian tradition in this area is still Augustine's question: can we properly value another person if we do not properly value ourselves as persons? And what does the decision to initiate one's own death say about one's self-perception as a person?

References

1   Augustine. *de civitate dei* **XIX**: iv
2   *Ibid* I: xix–xxvi, especially xix and xxi (on suicide and *magnitudo animi*)
3   *Ibid* **XIX**: iv, where self-preservation is described as 'the first and greatest imperative of nature', so that human beings should be reconciled to themselves . . . and make friends with themselves, so that they passionately want and seek to live as animals in whom soul and body are united'
4   Baker A. *Holy wisdom, or directions for the Prayer of Contemplation, methodically digested by R.F. Serenus Cressy*, Abbot Sweeney ed. London: Burns Oates and Washbourne, 1948: pp 633–4
5   An excellent recent discussion, in relation to a particular case in the USA, can be found in: Guroian V. *Ethics after Christendom. Toward an ecclesial Christian ethic*. Grand Rapids, MI: W.B. Eerdmans, 1994: pp 176–83
6   Hauerwas S. *Suffering presence. Theological reflections on medicine, the mentally handicapped, and the Church*. University of Notre Dame Press, 1986; and Edinburgh: T & T Clark 1988: p 93
7   Dostoyevsky F. *The Brothers Karamazov*, book 5, chapters 3 & 4
8   I refer again to Hauerwas, *op. cit.*, especially the essays on 'Religious concepts of brain death and associated problems' (pp 87–99) and 'Rational suicide and reasons for living' (pp 100–13). Behind much of this discussion, and other recent treatments lies Paul Ramsey's classic study, *The patient as person*. Yale University Press, 1970
9   Curiously, Karl Barth, in his *Church dogmatics* (III.4.55), discusses the question of war and violence under the rubric of 'The protection of life', taking as a starting point Albert Schweitzer's and Gandhi's philosophies–though he moves decisively away from them as the discussion proceeds. However, he acknowledges that he is deliberately using a non-traditional idiom in borrowing the language of the 'sanctity' of life

Euthanasia: Buddhist principles

Michael Barnes

Heythrop College, University of London, London, UK

Religions provide various forms of motivation for moral action. This chapter takes Buddhism as an example from within the Indian 'family' of religions and seeks to identify the doctrinal and cultural principles on which ethical decisions are taken. Although beginning from very different religious premises, it is argued that the conclusions to which Buddhism tends are broadly similar to those found within mainstream Christianity.

The debate about euthanasia within Buddhist circles is tentative and hung about with a suitably Buddhist reticence. Dr Raja Jayaweera's brief article in *Raft*, the journal of the Buddhist Hospice Trust, will serve as an introduction. Noting Buddha's constant exhortation to his disciples to subject all received teachings to careful critical analysis, he concludes that 'there is no official Buddhist position in relation to euthanasia or other similar moral problems. Seekers of the Buddhist position must simply apply the precepts and principles of the Dhamma and formulate their own views'[1].

'Official' positions may not exist but a few, albeit flawed, attempts to think through the questions consistently show that there is much more to Buddhist thinking on euthanasia than a purely pragmatic concern to keep the First Precept–not to take life–while practising the virtue of compassion. Thus Louis van Loon, arguing that in Buddhism 'volition constitutes a man's essential *beingness*', states that the value of human life is to be found in the capacity for conscious choice. In principle, therefore, the Buddhist would be in favour of '*voluntary* euthanasia, provided it applied within narrowly defined limits'[2]. Phillip Lecso, on the other hand, argues from the doctrine of *karma* that 'if the complete evolution of a karmic debt were to be disrupted by an active intervention on the part of the physician, it would then need to be faced again in a future existence'. His position is that Buddhism opts not for euthanasia but for hospice care[3]. Two very different emphases and two very different conclusions. The first, however, is only doubtfully Buddhist in its account of the human person; the second begs the question by failing to acknowledge that **any** treatment will have karmic consequences.

Contributors to the *Raft* symposium are not perplexed by the difficulty of providing Buddhist 'answers'. Several, in fact, note the danger in the

Postal address:
Fr Michael Barnes,
Heythrop College,
Kensington Square
London W8 5HQ, UK

very tendency to pin down a 'Buddhist position'. Thus Ajahn Sumedho: 'In using the advances of medicine and technology, what we really need is a kind of *reflective wisdom* which will help us to deal with particular problems as they arise, rather than attempting a kind of general doctrinal position about euthanasia – which is what Westerners tend to do'[4]. His point is that 'the Buddha-mind is not fixed on a position'; indeed a concern for 'moral positioning' can actually prevent a person from being fully responsible for his or her actions.

Such comments might give the impression that an inter-religious dialogue with Buddhism promises little by way of results. Certainly there is an enormous gap between the fundamental premises of Buddhism and the three Abrahamic 'religions of the Book'; wherever else Buddhism begins it is not with the concept of a creator God, still less with a people who are called by a special revelation. Buddhism insists on the autonomy of the moral subject. The precepts or 'rules of training' do not have the form of commands, like the Decalogue, but are undertakings expressed in the first person. At least in theory, one accepts voluntarily to follow the Buddha. Nevertheless, a fruitful dialogue between Buddhism and Christianity is taking place – even if this is, at the moment, largely confined to the more theological or metaphysical level[5]. The dialogue has naturally focused attention on 'common ground', noting in particular a convergence with regard to moral values, but has also recognised the importance of understanding the basic precepts and principles within their proper religious and cultural context – in the case of Buddhism within the complex world of Indian religion generally.

The contention of this chapter is that, once understood in this context, the dynamic motivating properly Buddhist action argues not for a moral relativism but for a convergence. While the sources of motivation are clearly different, the ethical conclusions to which they lead turn out to be remarkably similar to those which emerge from the mainstream of the Christian tradition.

Buddhism and Indian ascetical religion

Buddhism finds its origins in the 'renouncer movement' which flourished in northern India in the sixth century BCE. In its reaction to the Vedic sacrificial tradition of the time, and in its commitment to an ascetical way, early Buddhism has much in common with Jainism and the more orthodox movement within Brahmanism which led to the speculative Upaniṣads. But other factors were at work – notably a revaluation of the doctrine of *karma* in ethical terms.

In an enlightening article which sets out traditional Hindu views on euthanasia, Katherine Young remarks that the violence inherent in the warrior culture of the time was 'positively appropriated and converted into a religious path epitomized by non-violence and a fast to death, which ensured heaven or liberation'[6]. Jainism, with its concept of liberation as radical autonomy (*kaivalyam*), developed the practice of *ahimsā* (not just non-violence but the positive act of wishing well to all beings), and sanctioned the custom of *sallekhanā*, ritual fasting to death. This is the ultimate heroic act. Personal mortification is taken to its logical conclusion, so that the body is 'scoured out' (*sallikhita*) of its negative factors. The ascetic thus prepares for the decisive moment of death by making himself responsible for releasing the body from its bondage to matter. Given the religious constraints which surround and justify it this practice hardly fits the category of suicide; it is best described as a 'self-willed death'[7].

But does the very existence of such a concept within the cultural framework of Indian religion argue for a willingness at least to countenance euthanasia in certain cases? The reaction of the Buddha, as recorded in the ancient Theravāda tradition, is instructive. He always maintained immense respect for the high moral ideals of the Jains, but was critical of ascetical practices which failed adequately to address what he saw as the crucial problem. The dualism of the Jains was rejected. There are various examples in Buddhist texts of acts similar to the Jain *sallekhanā*. Some are quite bizarre, such as the case of the monk Godhika who achieved enlightenment at the moment he started to cut his throat[8]. But the position taken by the *Vinaya*, the rule of life for the monks, is clear. Once when the Buddha was away on retreat, his followers took rather too seriously the meditation on the impurity of the body. So intensely did they feel revulsion at the source of decay they experienced in themselves that many resolved to put an end to their lives. Others invoked the aid of a false monk called Migalaṇḍika who killed many monks in return for their robes and begging-bowls. The Buddha's response was to enact a precept which forbad such forms of suicide under the severest penalty – lifelong excommunication. Even the act of praising 'the beauty of death' or intentionally putting thoughts of death into someone's mind was strictly forbidden[9]. Such canonical texts would seem, therefore, to forbid any form of euthanasia.

The reason why the Buddha enacted the rule was to ensure that the pessimism of the age would not simply substitute the non-violence of the ascetic for the violence of the surrounding warrior-culture. The importance of an accurate 'diagnosis' of the human condition cannot be overstated. Without it the 'cure' will not be effective[10]. This is to be accomplished through the integrated practice of the Noble Eightfold Path, the key element of which – what gives it its peculiarly Buddhist character – is Mindfulness. Careful attention to the present moment avoids the all too human tendency to give a privileged status to particular experiences – even desirable states of peace and joy. It also warns against any act which might attempt to short-circuit the karmic process. According to the doctrine of *Karma*, which is found as a constant in all Indian religion, including Buddhism, deeds have results; a person is formed by his or her past. Not that in Buddhist terms this need lead to a fatalistic determinism. *Karma* may not be destroyed, as the Jains believed, by ascetical acts, but the *causes* of *Karma* can be identified and eradicated. Desire and ignorance in all their many and subtle forms are specifically noted. Even the minimal act of taking control in order to gain a 'self-willed death' sanctioned by the Jains is to be interpreted as, at best, a form of 'grasping', at worst, a type of escapism.

The ethic of intention

Buddhism seeks, therefore, to go to the root of the human problem by acknowledging that *Karma* – what binds us to the enslaving wheel of *Samsāra* – occurs in volition, at the point in the cognitive process where the individual directs him or herself to particular conscious acts. Intention thus plays a pivotal role in determining the moral status of an act; an action is immoral when it springs from mental states dominated by greed, hatred or delusion, moral when it proceeds from mental states characterised by opposite qualities. By attending, through the practice of Mindfulness, to those factors which condition present action, motivations are understood and intentions purified. This does not mean that actions are irrelevant. Rather, the moral quality of an act is to be determined by the interior state of the individual. By living according to the *Buddhadharma* one develops the 'skilful means' (*upāya*) by which evil *karma* is avoided and good *karma* practised.

In Buddhism, therefore, moral action and meditative practice are one – complementary ways of coming to terms with the radical impermanence to be found at the heart of human existence. Life is a process of coming to be and passing away; death and dying its most obvious manifestations. Hence the importance of preparing carefully for the moment of death, the quality of which will determine the next birth. As one Tibetan commentator puts it:

> Whichever of the two kinds of Karma dominates at the time of death determines one's next life . . . By forgetting or ignoring death one is unworthy of human existence, thinking only of the pleasures of this life. Lack of death awareness affects one's way of life and leads to regret at the time of death[11].

A human existence or rebirth is rare and precious – the most beneficial for attaining *Prajñā*, wisdom. Therefore, any action which might interfere with the final moments of that life must be treated with extreme caution. Putting it in somewhat negative terms, the ideal is to avoid the latent violence inherent in any attempt to dominate the dying process. More positively, according to the Tibetan model, the ideal is to die consciously, with a lucid awareness of what is happening. The Dalai Lama comments: 'from the Buddhist point of view, if a dying person has any chance of having positive, virtuous thoughts, it is important – and there is a purpose – for them to live even just a few minutes longer'[12]. Without *Prajñā* guiding all one's actions one always runs the risk of getting enmeshed in the karmic process of rebirth.

Wisdom and compassion

This should not, however, give the impression that some sort of 'principle of non-interference' betrays a callous lack of concern for the one who is dying. Such an emotionless attitude would be as unBuddhist as disrespect for the autonomy of the individual. Though the emphasis varies, in all Buddhist traditions the value of Compassion is set alongside Wisdom. The dying person will be accompanied by relatives and friends. They may be there to recite appropriate texts (the *Satipaṭṭhāna Sutta* in the Theravāda tradition or the *Bar-do Thos-grol* in the Tibetan) which will develop feelings of non-attachment in the dying person. But they will also be consciously projecting their own feelings of loving-kindness and compassion. Buddhism is nothing if not a religion of compassion, with a concern to alleviate the suffering of all sentient beings. An understanding of how the two values interact is crucial to an appreciation of Buddhist ethics.

Prajñā or Wisdom, seeing this conditioned world as it really is, means understanding that suffering is universal. The wise human being sees that everything is insubstantial and contingent; nothing exists independently of anything else. This is the truth of *Pratītyasamutpāda*, conditioned co-origination: all phenomena, and all sentient beings, arise and continue in dependence on others. But to come to terms with the source of suffering in one's own life through recognising its cause in acts of grasping and ideas of self-sufficiency is to become concerned for the same process happening in others. In fact, it makes little sense to talk of 'my' suffering as if it can be separated from 'yours'. *Sīla, Samādhi, Prajñā* – morality, concentration and wisdom, the 'three trainings' which summarise the Noble Eightfold Path – are interdependent.

Buddhist ethics entails much more, therefore, than a sort of preparatory prudential attitude – the necessary 'prelude' to enlightenment. After the Buddha was enlightened he spent the next 45 years preaching *Dharma*, out of compassion for sentient beings. His was the example which inspired the *bodhisattva* to work for the enlightenment of all, convinced that there can be no contradiction between the Wisdom which seeks one's own enlightenment and the Compassion which desires that of others. For the *bodhisattva* there is no purely individual enlightenment. Rather all are social beings; we are enlightened insofar as we are compassionate to others. Compassion will express itself in deeds which are concerned for the ultimate welfare of the other. The peculiar skill of the *bodhisattva* is the capacity to adapt such deeds to individual needs and circumstances. As Paul Williams puts it, 'the teaching of skilful means in Mahayana Buddhism comes to extend beyond simply adapting the doctrine to the level of the hearers to refer to any behaviour by the Buddha or Bodhisattvas which is perhaps not what one might expect, but which is done through the motivation of compassion, animated by wisdom, for the benefit of others'[13].

Using Buddhist principles

Buddhist ethics are motivated by a commitment to the First Precept and an instinct to behave compassionately towards all sentient beings. Such principles emerge from a religious culture which locates the moral value of human acts not in the specific results of the act but in the end or intention to which the act is directed. The overall intention is clear. 'Ideally body, speech and action all work harmoniously in accord with both ultimate and relative truth (*prajñā* and *karunā*)[14].' The Buddhist values a human life as a rare and precious opportunity to achieve *Nirvāna* – and, moreover, to make positive contributions towards the ultimate good of others. Such a positive respect for human life is the Buddhist equivalent of the Judaeo-Christian insistence on the God-given 'sanctity of life'. As Damien Keown puts it: 'the ultimate aim of Buddhism is to overcome death once and for all, and any affirmation of death or choice in favour of death is a rejection of this vision of human good'[15]. This is not, however, to insist that life must be preserved at all costs. Acceptance of the insubstantiality of all existence lies at the heart of both traditions. While both will refuse to sanction any deliberate attempt to destroy life, neither will insist that extraordinary means should be taken to preserve it.

In advocating a 'Middle Way' between extremes Buddhists do not opt for a *laissez-faire* liberalism. Principles are available; hard and fast answers are not. Buddhism is adaptable and ever-changing, but after more than 2000 years remains recognisably the same. The canonical sources witness not just to the wisdom of the founder but to the particular circumstances in which the key principles of his teaching were formed. Buddhists will still want to be faithful to a religious ethos in which all forms of violence are rejected – or at least their negative effects tempered by the virtue of compassion.

Acknowledgements

I wish to record my thanks to Bernard Hoose, Damien Keown and Ron Maddox for their helpful comments on this chapter.

References

1 Raja Jayaweera. Buddhism . . . a Middle Way? *Raft*: 1989–90; **2**: (Winter): p 3
2 van Loon L. A Buddhist viewpoint. In: Oosthuizen GC, Shapiro HA, Strauss SA. eds *Euthanasia*. Human Sciences Research Council Publication No 65. Cape Town: OUP, 1978: pp 73–9
3 Lesco PA. Euthanasia: a Buddhist perspective; *J Religion Health* 1986; **25**: 51–7
4 Interviewed in *Raft*, p 8 (emphasis added)
5 Keown D. Christian ethics in the light of Buddhist ethics. *Expository Times* 1995; **February**: 132–7
6 Young KK. Euthanasia: traditional Hindu views and the contemporary debate. In: Coward HG. ed. *Hindu ethics: purity, abortion and euthanasia*. New York: SUNY, 1989: pp. 71–118
7 Dundas P. *The Jains*. London: Routledge, 1992: especially pp 155f
8 Young KK *op. cit.* p 104. Young's discussion puts this and other particular cases of *mors voluntaria religiosa* in the widest possible religious context. The Indian religious tradition does not sanction forms of 'self-willed death'. She concludes, however, that there is a sharp demarcation between this and euthanasia understood as 'compassionate murder'.
9 Vinaya 3.70ff. The precept states: 'if any monk intentionally deprives a human being of life or looks for a knife-wielder he commits the offence of Defeat (*pārājika*) and is no longer in communion'. 'Knife-wielder' refers to the specific method of killing in this case, but the commentary makes it clear that the mode of killing is irrelevant. See the discussion of this and other similar texts from the Theravāda Pali tradition in: Keown D. *Buddhism and bioethics*. London: Macmillan, 1995: pp 167–87
10 The dynamic of the Buddha's first sermon with its Four Noble Truths – suffering, the cause of suffering, the end of suffering and the way to the end of suffering – lends itself to interpretation through a medical model. See Gombrich R. *Theravada Buddhism*. London: Routledge, 1988: p 5
11 Geshe Ngawang Dhargyey. *Tibetan tradition of mental development*. Dharamsala: Library of Tibetan Works and Archives, 1974: pp 54–5
12 Quoted in: Anderson P. Good death: mercy deliverance and the nature of suffering. *Tricycle, the Buddhist Review* 1992; **Winter**: 36–42
13 Williams P. *Mahāyāna Buddhism*. London: Routledge, 1989: p 144
14 Florida RE. Buddhism and the Four Principles. In: Gillon R. ed *Principles of health care ethics*. London: Wiley, 1994: p 108
15 Keown D. *Buddhism and bioethics op. cit.* p187

Euthanasia: sociological perspectives

Glennys Howarth* and **Margot Jefferys**[†]

*School of Cultural and Community Studies, University of Sussex, Brighton, UK and †Centre of Medical Law and Ethics, King's College London, London, UK

The potential of medicine to intervene to prolong or shorten the life of those considered to be dying or of those whose life is rated as of little or even negative value has only recently surfaced. It is an issue likely to affect society and the normative social relationships which that society believes it is its duty to promote. It is probable that, covertly, members of the medical profession have long played a role in speeding up the process of dying, with or without the consent of affected individuals. The openness, however, with which the moral issues involved in hastening or prolonging life by medical means are now discussed is a late 20th century phenomenon. Sociologists are beginning to study the circumstances surrounding the issues and the wider societal implications of possible changes in the law, professional practices and normative values. Their work may well begin to influence public policy as well as private practice.

Sociological approaches to ethical dilemmas

Have the disciplines of sociology or social anthropology a significant contribution to make to the understanding of euthanasia or to the current world-wide debate about the legitimacy and morality of its practice? This is the question which we consider in this chapter.

Sociologists are interested in the factors which lie behind the formation and maintenance of the normative and deviant judgements which are made about the morality of any form of human behaviour. They are open to the suggestion that some forms of behaviour attract such almost universal opprobrium that their repudiation constitutes an in-built requirement for the stability and survival of human groups. **In the main,** however, they seek explanations for observed variations in normative practices, beliefs and values.

Many, perhaps most, sociologists also hold strong beliefs about the morality of those end-of-life decisions which include euthanasia, however that term is defined. As scholars, however, they seek to separate their disciplinary approach to the subject from their personal predilections. In so far as they become protagonists in the contemporary debate on salient moral issues, they would claim to do so as citizens rather than as social scientists.

Correspondence to: Prof Margot Jefferys, Visiting Professor, Centre of Medical Law and Ethics, King's College, London, Strand, London WC2R 2LS, UK

A specifically sociological approach to euthanasia seeks to locate it within a general social, cultural, economic and political context. It would be seen as embedded in a particular set of functions governed by the accepted social *mores* for dealing with dying and death in any given society. The sociological assumption would be that the ways of relating to dying persons, which are seen as right and appropriate, reflect the society's dominant values and beliefs concerning life and death. The procedures associated with dying must also be compatible with the general moral standards accepted as normative. The rituals employed; the extent to which efforts may be made to hasten or postpone the moment of death, or deal with the physical pain and emotional distress experienced by survivors as well as the dying; the authority to act which is vested in those who claim expertise in curing or caring or in those who claim kinship with the dying person – all such matters are seen by sociologists as socially constructed.

Not surprisingly, those who are often called the founding fathers of sociology as an academic discipline threw little direct light on the specific practices surrounding death and dying in general, let alone euthanasia. However, some of the pioneers of social anthropology, who sought to understand the constants and the discontinuities in human social behaviour and beliefs, were fascinated by the ways in which death was perceived and treated in exotic societies, very different from their own industrialised post-enlightenment one[1]. These early social scientists, however, made some important observations about factors contributing to social solidarity and continuity and about the factors leading to social change. Durkheim, for example, made the important observation that the frequency of suicide (a form of end-of-life decision) in modern industrial societies was related to social structures and to the extent to which societies valued individual liberty as against social solidarity[2].

Why is euthanasia now on the agenda?

The ageing population and advances in medical technology

The absence to date of any substantial body of sociological work on euthanasia – defined here as measures designed to hasten or procure death – is not surprising. To begin with, the debate in western society about the morality and regulation of end-of-life decisions is itself relatively recent. It could result from the potentially destabilising effects on the collectivity of a new phenomenon – the survival of increasing numbers of very old or very handicapped individuals in its midst.

The reasons for the substantial shift in the age structure of populations are multiple and do not need to be detailed here. Briefly, they include economic growth and changes in the physical environment, life style and reproductive behaviour which began to accelerate, at least in the western world, in the 19th century[3]. In the second half of the 20th century, however, technological advances in the biomedical sciences and their application to human populations have also played a major part in the prolongation of life in general and in particular of lives which, in former times, as a result of injury or disease, would have ended much earlier than in old age[4].

The demonstrations of medical power over life and death have met with an ambivalent response, not least among members of the fraternity itself. We are now able to keep alive or resuscitate human beings whose continuing existence is valued neither by themselves nor by others. Should medicine always exercise this power? Or should it use its knowledge and authority to assist those who no longer wish to live (and those whose continued existence appears to absorb much of the community's resources which could be devoted to other valued objectives) to achieve a dignified death? In the changing social climate will older people feel increasing pressures on them to permit the withdrawal of life-sustaining measures? If doctors are believed to be willing to exercise their skills to procure death, will older people lose their faith in the intrinsic benevolence of the profession?

The holocaust

Most sociologists would agree with the proposition that the salience of the issues surrounding decisions to take human life has increased at least partly as a result of the horrific events of the 1930s and 1940s culminating in the holocaust. During that time, a minimum of 6 million Jews, and countless numbers of gypsies, mentally and physically disabled people and political dissidents were brutally and deliberately eliminated as a matter of state policy[5].

To suggest a resemblance between the specious justification of their deeds by the Nazis and the stance of those who argue that the lives of some individuals have become valueless to them and that in such circumstances they should be assisted, if they so wish, to end their existence, is grotesque. Comparing apparently diametrically opposed views on human dignity and autonomy could be regarded as no more than a debating ploy aimed at undermining the moral standing of the proponents of some form of legalised euthanasia by those who are not prepared to envisage the shortening of human life in any circumstances. Nevertheless, the spectre of a 'slippery slope' and of a potential travesty of humanitarian objectives if the state were to permit doctors to end lives in specific circumstances exercises a not inconsiderable influence on public opinion in general and legislators in particular[6]. The situation in The Netherlands, where doctors have such power, is being closely scrutinised in other western countries[7].

AIDS

A third phenomenon which has also helped to destabilise cultural presumptions about how death and dying should be treated has been the advent of AIDS-related illnesses. It has brought back the haunting spectre of inevitable death in early adulthood to those already identified as affected by HIV. Among them, at least in western countries, are young, middle class, intellectual and artistic individuals who want to take a full part in determining how their dying and death are managed[8].

The changing cultural milieu

The impact of revolutionary technological change on the way in which those of us alive today make sense of the world and our own individual identities within it is incalculable, and essentially paradoxical. There is the demonstrable power of modern technology to provide a very high proportion of the world's current population with a wealth of experiences which would have been unachievable fantasies for any human being who died before the end of the 19th century. The extension of our horizons in this way must be attributed to the development of scientific thought and its application to the tasks of satisfying insatiable human demands for 'the good life', however differently this may be conceived by individuals[9].

Nevertheless, the exponential changes which have already taken place in the last few decades have failed to satisfy the age-long human search for meaning[10]. Indeed, the irrelevance of scientific paradigms in pursuing the goal of ascribing meaning to human existence has triggered a variety of popular responses. One of these is a backlash against what is now seen as the tyranny of positivistic scientific thought and those identified as its orthodox proponents, including the medical profession[11]. In particular, there has been a growing popular desire in the last one or two decades to take management of dying out of the hands of professionals and, as far as possible, to enable dying people themselves to control end-of-life decision-making[12]. The strength of these desires is manifested in the increasing use of advance directives[13]; in the growing trend towards palliative care and for deaths to take place in hospices or with hospice support at home[14].

Recent sociological approaches to dying

Sociologists have in recent years begun to build a body of empirical evidence about how death and dying are handled in the contemporary world[15]. The observations they have made in hospitals and hospices have been used to make certain generalisations about what constitutes 'a good death' and what an unsatisfactory one. These studies have been supplemented by the systematic collection of accounts taken mostly after death from those believed to have been closest to or responsible for the dying person[16]. Most of these studies have not tackled directly the issue of euthanasia; but one recent study in the UK invited relatives to say whether they and the dead person would have wished for death to have taken place earlier than it in fact did[17].

Awareness of the pain and suffering (psychological as well as physical) which, it is usually assumed, the process of dying involves has been a major deterrent to sociologists collecting data about it. To obtain information and so understand the experience of dying, sociologists would ideally like to observe it as it is being experienced first hand. More and more human behaviours or attributes are now seen as legitimate ones to question individuals about, if not to observe. At one time, it was not permissible for social survey researchers to ask individuals about their age or income. Now it is not uncommon for people to agree to provide researchers with information about their sexual behaviour, including the frequency of intercourse or the number of partners and/or orgasms they have had in a given period of time.

There is reluctance, however, to invade the physical and temporal space around the dying person which is seen as legitimately occupied exclusively by kin, close friends and professional carers. There may also be a fear of confrontation with a situation which challenges the capacity for emotional self-control and may act as an unwelcome reminder of personal mortality. The reasons for such reluctance are not difficult to understand. Given increasing concern to protect patients from what might be interpreted as intrusion, it is unlikely to change much in future[18].

The result is that systematic evidence about the emotional responses experienced by dying people has been largely secondhand[19]. One notable exception is a recent study carried out, like most other studies of dying, with people dying of cancer[20]. Most research, however, has had to rely on the accounts of kin or professional carers after the death. The studies are of variable quality and reflect, among other things, the degree of warmth and understanding which existed between the informant and the dead person. Other kinds of account – for example those from individuals who claim to have experienced a resurrection – are, if not suspect, so unusual as not to be entitled to any form of generalisation. So too are accounts given by mediums who claim to put living relatives in touch with their dear departed.

It is likely that obtaining firsthand coherent accounts of those who are dying and might wish to exercise the choice of dying earlier by being able to call on their professional carers or relatives to help them will continue to be difficult. Indeed, it is possible that, given age trends in mortality, more of those dying in the future than at present will be suffering from some degree of dementia at the time and hence not regarded as competent to express an opinion[21]. The still uncertain prospects for AIDS mortality may modify this prediction.

Agencies in the determination of euthanasia practices and policies

One of the main interests of sociologists is in what they call 'agency', a term which has a broader meaning for them than it has for lawyers[22]. By it they mean the social institution which has by legal authority or common consent the recognised right to set and control the normative practice in any given field of human activity. In the case of end-of-life decisions, the agency is shared and the desirability of the power distribution between actual and potential agents is disputed. Indeed, the current debate on euthanasia is at least partly about agency, about who does and who should control the decisions to hasten or procure death.

The medical profession

In western societies, the major agent in end-of-life decisions is the medical profession. Public perceptions of the technical competence of its members and the widespread desire of those in vulnerable situations to endow them with superior dispassionate moral values give them a high degree of popular licence to take problematic, uncomfortable decisions[23]. Nevertheless, individual members of the profession, although frequently faced with the responsibility of taking measures which may shorten or prolong life, have had little if any formal instruction in how to consider the ethical or legal questions intrinsically involved in the decision making. Consequently, their actions reflect individual beliefs, those of the caring teams with whom they work, and their perceptions of the law and of the wishes of the dying person's next-of-kin and of the dying person her or himself, rather than any generally accepted professional stance. This *pot pourri* may well lead to different outcomes in clinically similar situations.

Representative bodies of doctors have aired the issues and taken positions on some of the ethical and procedural ones[24]. But the enormity of the task, when stated bluntly, of 'playing God', has made many members of the profession and its leaders call for firmer guidance if not direction from legislators or from judges on how and when individual doctors should exercise their powers[25].

Priests and religious leaders

In western, secular societies, priests of the major Christian religious traditions are fighting a losing battle to retain the popular authority on such questions which they once indubitably held. They are less powerful than they once were to influence the outcome of the debate about the legitimacy and regulation of different ways of handling the desires and fears of dying people. Nevertheless, to a greater or lesser extent, they are protagonists of particular viewpoints which they seek to reconcile with the basic tenets of their faith. The Roman Catholic church in particular still exercises, directly or indirectly, considerable influence on decisions whether to sustain the life of new-borns with only the prospect of a short, restricted existence requiring dedicated sacrifice from kin and carers and substantial opportunity costs to the community[26].

The media

The media, too, must be counted another independent agent or force of considerable contemporary weight. Responding to multiple influences from their customers – namely their readers, viewers, listeners and advertisers – as well as from their governing bodies, they engage increasingly if not always over-scrupulously in activities designed to draw more and more people into the arena where moral and ultimately political issues are debated[27].

The power of the media to persuade health authorities and government effectively to ignore priorities (often set up to ensure that 'cinderella' services are adequately funded) in favour of expensive procedures designed to save the life of a single individual (with a probably negligible disability-free life-years' expectation) is exercised relatively frequently[28]. Unfortunately, the media seldom recognise explicitly any obligation to present their audiences with a full enough picture of the issues to ensure that public opinion is truly informed.

Pressure groups

Other groups representing particular widely held opinions, such as the sanctity of life in all circumstances[29], or, conversely, the 'natural' right of individuals to ask for assistance in ending a painful existence[30], have also become significant actors seeking to exercise an influence on public opinion and, possibly, on the legislative framework governing end-of-life decisions.

The wider social implications of societal arrangements for end-of-life decision-making

In this paper, we have pointed to the general factors, demographic, technological, economic and cultural, which, as sociologists, we believe are responsible for the present public manifestation of intensifying interest in euthanasia. We have suggested that the social agencies involved are either those assigned a major role in the management of dying, or those regarded as guardians or interpreters of the moral standards of the society. The media facilitate the exchange of opinions and in doing so act as agents of either change or reinforcement of traditional values.

As sociologists, however, we would also stress the interconnectedness of societal beliefs and practices concerning death and dying and those to do more generally with issues of the autonomy and conversely of the dependency of individuals.

Dependency and autonomy

The issue of dependency is intimately bound up with that of euthanasia. In one of the few studies to address such issues through the medium of next-of-kin informants, the desire to speed up the end of life appeared to be related to feelings about the loss of independence in everyday living[17]. Such feelings were said to be felt by both the dying person and her or his relative or friend.

Indeed, there is a cultural abhorrence of relying on others to provide care, particularly in the most personal and intimate tasks of daily living. In modern societies which place a high value on reciprocity in relationships as well as on autonomy[31], adult dependency is regarded as undignified, leading to a loss of self-esteem by those requiring care, no matter how willingly or lovingly administered[32]. Moreover, the dependency of one person on another, if accepted, inevitably involves a reduction of choice and hence of autonomy on the part of that other. Although studies have shown that the dependency of an elderly, frail person is in most instances accepted – and in many instances is seen to bring its own rewards – there is none the less a growing consciousness that the decision to accept that dependency could be construed as yielding to a form of moral blackmail[33]. The success of the blackmail is the product of a strong fear of adverse social judgements, whether or not such a fear is justified.

The advance directive or living will is an attempt on the part of individuals to insure their autonomy in circumstances in which their dependency on others may reach a level which they consider unacceptable. The impact of a great extension in the practice of giving doctors advance directives requesting them to withhold life-prolonging measures, particularly if the directives were to acquire statutory sanction, is likely to affect the customary doctor–patient relationship, and particularly the balance of autonomy and dependency between the parties. If the practice were to become general rather than rare and involve asking a relative or friend to sanction or procure an earlier death, it would also in all probability signal a change in the nature of inter-generational, kin relationships.

Acknowledgements

We would like to thank Ann Cartwright, Joanna Haynes and Eric Scowen who read an earlier draft of the paper and made useful suggestions which we have incorporated into the text.

References

1   Frazer JG. *The belief in immortality and the worship of the dead.* London: Macmillan, 1913; Tylor EB. *Primitive culture. Researches into the development of mythology, religion, art and custom.* 2 Vols. London: John Murray, 1871

2   Durkheim E. *Suicide: a study in sociology.* Spalding JA, Simpson G. trans. London: Routledge Kegan Paul, 1952

3   McKeown T. *The modern rise of population.* New York: Academic Press, 1976

4   Szreter S. The importance of social intervention in Britain's mortality decline, c 1850–1914: a reinterpretation of the role of public health. *Soc Hist Med* 1988 1: 1–33

5   Weindling P. *Health, race and German politics between national unification and Nazism 1875–1945.* London: Cambridge University Press, 1989; Burleigh M. *Death and deliverance: 'euthanasia' in Germany 1900–1945.* London: Cambridge University Press, 1994

6   Dworkin R. *Life's dominion. An argument about abortion and euthanasia.* London: Harper Collins, 1993

7   Gomez CF. *Regulating death: euthanasia and the case of The Netherlands.* Basingstoke: Macmillan, 1991

8   Small N. Dying in a public place: AIDS deaths. In: Clark D. ed. *The sociology of death.* Oxford: Blackwell, 1993

9   Porter D, Porter R. (eds) *Doctors, politics and society; historical essays.* Amsterdam: Rodopi, 1993

10 Nagel T. *Mortal questions* London: Cambridge University Press, 1979 and Bauman Z. *Mortality, immortality and other life strategies.* Cambridge: Polity, 1992

11 Illich I. *Limits to medicine.* London: Marion Boyars, 1976; also e.g, 'Caduceus', Issues No. 14 and 27. *Quarterly Journal.* Leamington Spa: Caduceus Publications, 1991, 1995

12 Kelner MJ, Bourgeault IL. Patient control over dying: responses of health care professionals. *Soc Sci Med* 1993; **36**, 6: 757–65; Walter T. *The revival of death.* London: Routledge, 1994

13 British Medical Association. *Advance statements about medical treatment. Code of Practice.* London: BMJ Publishing Group, 1995; Hoefler JM. *Death right: culture, medicine, politics and the right to die.* Westview Press, 1994

14 Field D, James N. Where and how people die. In: Clark D. ed. *The future for palliative care.* Buckingham: Open University Press, 1993

15 See, Field D. *Nursing the dying.* London: Tavistock Routledge, 1989; Glaser BG, Strauss AL. *Awareness of dying.* Chicago: Aldine, 1965; Hockey J. *Experiences of death.* Edinburgh: Edinburgh University Press, 1990; Prior L. *The social organization of death.* Basingstoke: Macmillan, 1989; Sudnow D. *Passing on.* New Jersey: Prentice-Hall, 1967; Williams RA. *Protestant legacy.* Oxford: Oxford University Press, 1990

16 Bowling A, Cartwright A. *Life after a death.* London: Tavistock, 1982

17 Seale C, Addington-Hall J. Dying at the best time. *Soc Sci Med* 1995; **40**: 589–95

18 National Health Service Training Division. *Standards for Local Ethical Research Ethics Committee. A framework for ethical review.* London: NHS Executive Board, 1994; Royal College of Physicians. *Research involving patients.* London: RCP, 1990

19 Kubler-Ross E. *On death and dying.* New York: Macmillan, 1969

20 Kellehear A. *Dying of cancer: the final years of life.* Chur: Harwood Academic, 1990

21 Law Commission. *Mental incapacities Item 9 of the Fourth Programme of Law Reform: mentally incapacitated adults.* Law Commission No 231, London: HMSO, 1995

22 Berger PL, Luckmann T. *The social construction of reality.* London: Allen Lane, Penguin Press, 1967; Archer M. *Culture as agency.* London: Cambridge University Press, 1988

23 Anderson JG, Caddell DP. Attitudes of medical professionals toward euthanasia. *Soc Sci Med* 1993; **37**: 105–14

24 British Medical Association. *Euthanasia.* London: BMA, 1988

25 House of Lords. *Report of the Select Committee on Medical Ethics.* (HL paper 21), Vol 1. London: HMSO, 1994

26 Pope John Paul. *Evangelium vitae.* Vatican City: 11th Encyclical, March 1995

27 See, Democratisation of death. *The Independent,* 16 March 1995; Lambert S. Filming the last taboo. *The Independent,* 17 March 1995

28 See, for example, the case of child B denied further treatment for leukaemia on the NHS by the Cambridge Health Authority. The case was extensively treated in the press between 10–15 March 1995

29 Society for the Protection of the Unborn Child (SPUC)

30 Voluntary Euthanasia Society

31 Qureshi H, Walker A. *The caring relationship: elderly people and their families.* Basingstoke: Macmillan, 1989

32 Seale C, Addington-Hall J. Euthanasia: the role of good care. *Soc Sci Med* 1995; **40**: 581–7

33 Lewis J, Meredith B. *Daughters who care: daughters caring for mothers at home.* London: Routledge Kegan Paul, 1988

Recent historical perspectives regarding medical euthanasia and physician assisted suicide

Demetra M Pappas

Center for Biomedical Ethics, University of Minnesota, Minnesota, USA and Departments of Law and Sociology, London School of Economics, London, UK

Medical assistance in the termination of life, whether euthanasia or assisted suicide, is arguably one of the most hotly debated topics as we approach the millenium. While euthanasia has been a subject of controversy for thousands of years, the historical influences *vis à vis* the medical profession are primarily rooted in the past century.

This chapter seeks to explore some of the recent historical developments which have had an impact on the emergence of medical euthanasia and physician assisted suicide. The objective is to juxtapose events in a way that relates historical fact (and fiction) to current events and debates. Sociology, law and theology have each a view and impact in this arena; however, they are deliberately left to the side, so as to allow for a longitudinal landscape.

'Medical aid in dying', a term which euphemises the concept of medical assistance in the termination of life, embraces the practices of both euthanasia (as performed by members of the health care team) and physician assisted suicide. It has arguably become the most important issue facing the medical profession (and a number of those having a relation to medicine, including law, bioethics, sociology, and theology to name but a few). Axiomatic to developing a historical perspective of medical euthanasia is the definition of history as the 'continuous methodical record of important or public events . . . the study of past events, especially of human affairs'[1]. Thus, accepting that history is the record of human society, the first difficulty in developing a historical perspective on medical euthanasia is the fact that essays advocating active euthanasia in the context of modern medicine first appeared in the US and England in the 1870s[2], notwithstanding millenia of debate of the topic in other disciplines[3].

This should not be seen as too surprising given that the modern hospital is considered to have existed for approximately 100 years and that its function and efficacy have changed dramatically. Hoefler and Kamoie observe that before the turn of the century, there existed patient mortality rates of 25% and medical staff mortality rates of 10% per year;

Postal address:
Demetra M Pappas Esq,
Center for Biomedical
Ethics, University of
Minnesota, University
Office Plaza, Suite 110,
2221 University
Avenue SE, Minneapolis,
MN 55414-3074, USA

many members of both groups succumbed to acute infections derivative of their presence, rather than their role, in hospitals[4]. Thus, the birth of the modern American (medical) euthanasia controversy, since placed around the year 1890[5], coincides with the modernization of medicine. Therefore, in considering medical aid in dying, this exploration of the historical perspectives ultimately finds itself rooted in the early part of this century, although events before this time have relevance.

Modernization of medicine

It is said that with the modernization of medicine, medicine has replaced religion as the major institutional moulder of cultural death fears and immortality desires. This is because modern medicine, like religion and the law, seeks to discover, control and eradicate undesirable elements[6]. Breakthroughs of the past century have empowered doctors to battle acute infection successfully, thus transforming the hospital, from functioning essentially as a hospice, to an institution which provides medical, surgical and curative treatment for the sick and injured. Technological advancements have further armed the medical profession, enabling success in the battle against untimely deaths brought on by failing organs. The roles of doctors in relation to the dying bear even less similarity to their counterparts of two centuries ago than do the hospitals.

Consider, for example, how doctors were involved with hastening the death of George Washington, the first President of the US. In 1799, President Washington developed a sore throat; his doctors, in the two days before his death bled 5 pints of blood from him, in accordance with the then state-of-the-art of medicine. Washington's death was probably (and obviously inadvertently) as likely to have been caused by shock and loss of blood as by strep throat (for which he also gargled)[7]. This may well have been the first publicised (though not prosecuted) 'assisted death' by a physician in America. Of course, in the present day, Washington would have received any number of antibiotics, retained his life-blood, and likely lived to die of one of the degenerative diseases now common to old age.

With the defeat of acute disease, degenerative illness, also coming into prominence at the end of the 19th and beginning of the 20th centuries, fuelled the beginnings of the modern medical euthanasia controversy. The increasing prominence of degenerative and late onset illnesses is, of course, consistent with the societal changes, whereby life expectancy has doubled from the norm of 40 years in 1851[8].

Consider, for instance, that between 1886 and 1913, cancer deaths in the New England and Mid-Atlantic areas of the US rose from 41 per

100,000 to 90 per 100,000. Cancer served as the paradigm chronic and degenerative disease referent for discussions of suicide and euthanasia in the early 1900s. One early example of this, on the cusp of the current century, was an 1899 editorial in *The Lancet*, advising a physician that in the use of morphine and chloroform to relieve the pain of a patient with ovarian cancer:

> We consider that a practitioner is perfectly justified in pushing such treatment to an extreme degree, if that is the only way of affording freedom from acute suffering . . . [and] we are of the opinion that even should death result, the medical man has done the best he can for his patient[9].

Thus, the introduction of the concept of the double effect of medication as a response to intolerable degenerative disease has an introduction into mainstream, modern medical practice. Perhaps unsurprisingly, also around that time, the first proposal (in the Western world) for legalizing medical euthanasia was made (and rejected) in 1905 in the state of Ohio; after this time, during which a proposal was also made and defeated in Iowa, no further proposals were made in the US until 1937[10].

This gives perspective to much of the activity in the modern medical aid in dying movement, as well as to the increased publicity about and **by** doctors who engage in medical euthanasia. Pressure groups who devoted time and economic support to the campaigns in America to legalize medical aid in dying in Washington State (failed *Proposition Initiative 119* in 1991) and medical euthanasia in California (*California State Terminal Illness Assistance in Dying Initiative 161* in 1992) were heavily supported in time and money by the AIDS lobbies. Likewise, one heavily publicised witness at the 4 March 1994 public hearing of the Michigan Commission on Death and Dying was a 37-year-old woman who had what she testified to as 'a 97% probability of developing Huntington's disease', a fatal degenerative neurological illness of a 10–20 year duration.

Thus, it is readily apparent that because opportunistic and acute illnesses which would have resulted in death are now treatable, parades of horrors emerge as the central vehicle of death (with related syndromes and derivative infections likewise nearly as controllable as acute diseases). The inevitable result is that our concept of illness, as well as our perspective of how to manage it, has changed radically. However, not only are the doctors' powers expanded, but patients' roles and rights are, with a heavy emphasis on patient autonomy and family participation in health care decisions.

Renegotiating death

If doctors in the past were left to watch helplessly (or arguably inadvertently hasten) the deaths of their patients, then modern medicine, with its treatments and cures, has been accompanied in the 1900s by a more interactive relationship between the medical profession and its clientele. Contrast George Washington's death with that of King George V in 1936. It is said that the King's personal physician, Lord Dawson of Penn, allegedly having ascertained that Queen Mary 'saw no virtue in allowing the King's suffering to continue', took whatever steps were needed to cut it short[11].

This event coincided with the year in which the then-recently formed Voluntary Euthanasia Society (1932) initiated *The Voluntary Euthanasia (Legislation) Bill* in the House of Lords 'to legalize under certain conditions the administration of euthanasia to persons desiring it and who are suffering from illness of a fatal and incurable character involving severe pain'. This 1936 Bill, and a subsequent motion introduced some years later (in 1950) for an investigation by the House of Lords into the matter of legalizing voluntary euthanasia, were both defeated[12]. These events were closely paralleled in the US by the birth of the Euthanasia Society of America and the unsuccessful introduction, also in 1936, of proposed legislation in Nebraska.

A principal objection common to the proposals on both sides of the Atlantic Ocean, raised in response to the 1930s proposals to allow for voluntary euthanasia, the 1970s and 1980s right to die legislation and the 1990s medical aid in dying bills, has been that the 'thin edge of the wedge', will be skated by allowing for any hastening of death[13]. In short, the wedge argument asserts that once there is one allowance for euthanasia, in even the most seemingly innocuous and compassionate of circumstances, further legislation or case precedent will allow for an ultimate breakdown of accepted legal standards and medical ethics. While there was no object example to be cited during the early half of this century, many now draw attention to the lessons to be learned from the Nazi euthanasia programme.

Historical perspectives of Nazi doctors and euthanasia

Courts making precedent setting decisions, legislative committees making recommendations to governments, and doctors and medical ethicists making hospital policy all look to learn from the historical lessons of the Nazi experience. That period is held to be the paradigmatic example of the slippery slope from the voluntary to the most grotesquely involuntary of euthanasia programmes, abuse of medical technology, and erosion of traditional medical ethics. The Nazi euthanasia programme serves as a powerful example of the difference between historical fact and historical truth.

The concept of the elite precipitating the movement for (and deriving the benefit from) euthanasia is, in actuality, a source of the original Nazi euthanasia programme, 'the blessing of [which] was only to be granted to [true] Germans'[14]. The notorious 'euthanasia Aktion T4' regarding the killing of the mentally ill and handicapped in 1940 and 1941 and 'Aktion 14 f 3', which led to the involuntary 'medical' euthanasia of some 275,000 people, were actually – as a matter of law – criminal in nature, whereas voluntary euthanasia, as originally contemplated had been **rejected** by the Nazi dominated Reichstag in 1933.

The nationwide policy of administering euthanasia to mentally defective people, psychotics, epileptics, those 'suffering' from old age and its related infirmities and organic neurological disorders (and later Jews, foreigners, members of other races, homosexuals, and other 'impure' people) was in violation of the national penal code and prompted the Minister of Justice to demand (unsuccessfully) its cessation. As for German doctors and medical students who opposed the National Socialist party, those who were unable to flee into the army to remove themselves from this conflict of duties found themselves facing 'elimination'[15].

One recent review of the cases of doctors who participated in the programme concludes that not only did many doctors participate with impunity (i.e. they were not indicted at Nuremberg), but in fact 'profited from the unique opportunity to experiment on living human beings, and they supported the Nazi utopian view of a society cleansed of everything sick, alien, and disturbing . . .'[16]. These doctors are described as 'average' physicians in terms of their attitude, thinking and daily routine, whose diaries and journals have come to light only in the past 10 years, stirring great debate among members of the German medical profession. In stark contrast, as noted by Humphry and Wickett, there is no record of the Nazi doctors either killing or assisting in the suicide of a patient who was suffering intolerably from a fatal illness[17].

It is a curious aside that where many indicate a profound reservation, properly expressed, that the wedge, or the slippery slope from voluntary to non-voluntary (as in persistent vegetative state) to involuntary euthanasia is exemplified by the Nazi era, the first full-scale study in English of the Nazi 'euthanasia' programme was published in 1994[18]. Moreover, Arthur Caplan, now Director of the Center for Bioethics at the University of Pennsylvania Medical Center, wrote that it took him more than a decade to organize a 2-day conference to examine the Meaning of the Holocaust for Bioethics at the University of Minnesota,

Center for Biomedical Ethics[19]. Professor Caplan raises the question of why it was that 'bioethics had paid so little attention to the obvious dilemma raised by the reality that Nazi doctors and scientists had grounded their actions [generally, but easily arguably with regard to euthanasia] in moral language and ethical justifications'[20]. Caplan's collection, like the book by Burleigh, sought to fill what the former called a 'huge and inexcusable gap in the literature'. Perhaps the reason the historical facts of the Nazi euthanasia programme have been under-reported and the historical truth underdeveloped is that the historical perspective is so frankly anomalous as to render juxtapositions of the present day case studies to historical analogies a nullity[21]. It must be hoped that the reason for the gaps, now filled, is that the concepts addressed have more to do with historical perspectives of war than of medicine, notwithstanding the impact of the Nazi euthanasia programme on the post-war euthanasia cases, debate and movement.

Euthanasia in the post war period

Glanville Williams, arguing in the late 1950s that permissive legislation regarding euthanasia (assisted suicide not having been introduced as a concept in medico-legal circles at that time), suggested that the 'purpose of such legislation would be to set doctors free from their fear of the law so that they can think only of the relief of their patients [and that] one result of the measure that doctors would welcome is that by legalizing euthanasia it would bring the whole subject within ordinary medical practice'[22]. Cases such as those of Dr Hermann Sander, prosecuted (and acquitted) in New Hampshire in 1950 after he administered four injections of air into the arm of his patient, in circumstances strikingly similar to the 1992 Winchester Crown court prosecution (and suspended sentence) of rheumatologist Dr Nigel Cox, would lend credence to the belief, even in the absence of polls, that there was a long held silent practice.

The legal profession has allowed the medical profession wide latitude in such cases. In the UK, the prosecution of Dr John Bodkin Adams, who was acquitted in a spare 44 minutes, led to the establishment of a jury instruction (adopted in legislation in several jurisdictions) regarding 'double effect'. This defence asserts that the treatment was medically appropriate (for instance, to relieve pain), but that the death was hastened as a result of the medication.

A modern (but highly controversial) usage of this concept (which in theory is allowed by theologians as an extension, and by lawyers as an exception, to the sanctity of life principle) was demonstrated in the celebrated trial of Dr Jack Kevorkian in 1994 in Michigan. Dr Kevorkian, a former pathologist, who as of the date of this writing has assisted in some 25 suicides of terminally and chronically ill people, argued that a jury should not find him guilty of assisting in a suicide (a crime the Michigan Legislature created specifically in response to Dr Kevorkian's activities), because the carbon monoxide he administered to the deceased was the only thing he could think of to use to alleviate his suffering. Dr Kevorkian, who was acquitted after less than 8 hours of deliberations, continues to assist in suicides.

Conclusions

This chapter sought to provide a historical perspective to the current medical aid in dying debate and to consider some of the forces which have come into play over the past century. Most events can be credibly argued as providing either historical precedent or supporting a theory of present historicism. Additionally, advances in medical technology and the retreat of acute illness as a cause of death have left the residual question of when death is appropriate in cases of degenerative illness. Because legal and ethical concepts do not always follow apace of technological advances, perspective may perhaps be the most elusive aspect of the emergence of a concept of medical aid in dying, be it called euthanasia, assisted suicide or assistance in the termination of life. That, however, will best be evaluated in the future.

References

1   Hawkins JM. ed. *The Oxford paperback dictionary*. 3rd edn. Oxford: Oxford University Press, 1990: p 383

2   This is nearly contemporaneous with the emergence of eugenics, a concept defined in 1883 by Francis Galton, the British scientist, with reference to a scientific and social movement whereby better breeding could be effected by manipulating heredity. Stepan NL. *The hour of eugenics: race, gender and nation in Latin America*. Ithaca: Cornell University Press, 1991: pp 1–2 (citing Davenport CB. *Heredity in relation to eugenics&D*. New York: Henry Holt, 1911: p 1)

3   New York State Task Force on Life and the Law. *When death is sought: assisted suicide and euthanasia in the medical context*. 1994: pp 77, 82. Since other chapters in this issue address those perspectives relating to theological history, they will not be discussed further here

4   Hoefler JM, Kamoie BE. *Deathright: culture, medicine, politics and the right to die*. Colorado: Westview Press, 1994: p 67 (citing Bronzino JD, Smith JD, Vincent H, Maurice L. *Medical technology and society: an interdisciplinary perspective*. Cambridge: MIT Press, 1990: p 9). Hoefler and Kamoie, after citing these astonishing statistics, go on to attribute subsequent reduced hospital mortality rates to Florence Nightingale's crusade against unsanitary conditions in hospitals, which was waged during the 1880s, before which they relegate hospitals to being primarily religious and charitable places for warehousing the sick and the poor.

5   Kuepper SL. *Euthanasia in America, 1890–1960: the controversy, the movement and the law.* Unpublished PhD dissertation. Rutgers University, The State University of New Jersey at New Brunswick, 1981: p 56, n 84

6   Kearl MC. *Endings: a sociology of death and dying.* Oxford: Oxford University Press, 1989: p 406

7   Hoefler JM, Kamoie BE. *op. cit.* pp 46–7

8   Taylor S. Approaches to health and health care. In: Taylor S, Field D. eds. *Sociology of health and health care: an introduction for nurses.* Oxford: Blackwell, 1993: pp 43–4

9   Emanuel EJ. Euthanasia, historical, ethical and empiric perspectives. *Arch Intern Med* 1994; **154**: 1890-1 (citing Editorial. Euthanasia. *Lancet* 1899; **1**: 532

10 Tsarounas A. The case against assisted suicide. *Ohio N Univ L Rev* 1993; **20**: 793, 796 (citations omitted)

11 Barrington MR. Euthanasia: an English perspective. In: Berger AS, Berger J. eds. *To die or not to die? Cross-disciplinary, cultural and legal perspectives on the right to choose death.* New York: Prager, 1990: p 87

12 For a thorough discussion of these events, see Williams G. *The sanctity of life and the criminal law.* London: Faber & Faber, 1958: pp 293–311

13 This should be distinguished from the theological objection which is that the sanctity of life must not be violated by the taking of human life, through medical euthanasia, physician assisted suicide, or otherwise, even where there is a compassionate motivation

14 Kamisar Y. Euthanasia legislation: some non-religious objections. In: Downing AB, Smoker B. eds. *Voluntary euthanasia: experts debate the right to die.* London: Peter Owen, 1986: p 140

15 British Medical Association. *Euthanasia.* London: BMA, 1988 (citing Hanauske-Abel HM. From Nazi holocaust to nuclear holocaust: a lesson to learn? *Lancet* 1986; **ii**: 271–3)

16 Pross C. Nazi doctors, German medicine and historical truth. In: Annas GJ, Grodin MA. *The Nazi doctors and the Nuremberg code: human rights in human experimentation.* New York: Oxford University Press, 1992: p 38 and generally at pp 32–52

17 Humphry D, Wickett A. *The right to die. Understanding euthanasia.* New York: Harper & Row, 1986: p 23

18 Burleigh M. *Death and deliverance: euthanasia in Germany 1900–1945.* Cambridge: Cambridge University Press, 1994

19 Caplan AL. ed. *When medicine went mad: bioethics and the holocaust.* Totowa, NJ: Humana Press, 1992: preface p vi

20 *Id.*

21 On the other hand, it is noteworthy that in the USA, the first euthanasia society, the Euthanasia Society of America, was formed in 1938, but set aside its efforts to promote legislation during World War II because of reports of the Nazi practice

22 *The sanctity of life and the criminal law. op. cit.,* p 305

Index

Biological psychiatry

Scientific Editor

Eve C Johnstone